Teaching
the Bible to
Adults and Youth

Creative Leadership Series

Assimilating New Members, Lyle E. Schaller
Beginning a New Pastorate, Robert G. Kemper
The Care and Feeding of Volunteers, Douglas W. Johnson
Creative Stewardship, Richard B. Cunningham
Time Management, Speed B. Leas
Your Church Can Be Healthy, C. Peter Wagner
Leading Churches Through Change, Douglas Alan Walrath
Building an Effective Youth Ministry, Glenn E. Ludwig
Preaching and Worship in the Small Church,
William Willimon and Robert L. Wilson
Church Growth, Donald McGavran and George G. Hunter III
The Pastor's Wife Today, Donna Sinclair
The Small Town Church, Peter J. Surrey
Strengthening the Adult Sunday School Class, Dick Murray
Church Advertising, Steve Dunkin
Women as Pastors, edited by Lyle E. Schaller
Leadership and Conflict, Speed B. Leas
Church Finance in a Complex Economy, Manfred Holck, Jr.
The Tithe, Douglas W. Johnson
Surviving Difficult Church Members, Robert D. Dale
Your Church Has Personality, Kent R. Hunter
The Word on Families, G. William Sheek
Five Audiences, Warren J. Hartman
How to Build a Magnetic Church, Herb Miller
Teaching the Bible to Adults and Youth, Dick Murray

Teaching the Bible to Adults and Youth

Dick Murray

Creative Leadership Series
Lyle E. Schaller, Editor

Abingdon Press/Nashville

TEACHING THE BIBLE TO ADULTS AND YOUTH

Library of Congress Cataloging-in-Publication Data

MURRAY, DICK, 1924–
    Teaching the Bible to adults and youth.

    (Creative leadership series)
    Bibliography: p. 171
    1. Bible—Study.   I. Title.   II. Series.
BS600.2.M87   1987   220'.07   87-1815

ISBN 0-687-41082-7
(alk. paper)

MANUFACTURED BY THE PARTHENON PRESS AT
NASHVILLE, TENNESSEE, UNITED STATES OF AMERICA

To the Bible classes
to whom I owe much
at Hyde Park, New York,
Hooks, Texas, and Houston, Texas

and

To my children by birth
and marriage: Ruth, Martin,
Walter, Louise,
and their children,
Martin Thomas and Matthew

Foreword

More adults were engaged in serious continuing Bible study groups in the United States in 1986 than ever before in American history. Although it is impossible to prove that statement since the detailed statistics are not available, that appears to be the picture.

The highly visible difference between 1986 and 1956 or 1896 is that today most of these classes are not meeting in church buildings on Sunday morning. Instead, people today are gathering in homes on Tuesday evening or in boardrooms in downtown office buildings at seven o'clock in the morning or in church buildings at two o'clock on Thursday afternoon or at eight o'clock on Saturday morning or in high school cafeterias before school begins or in hospital meeting rooms at midnight or in camps throughout the summer.

The mid-1950s marked the peak years of Sunday school attendance in scores of denominations. During the past three decades Bible study, to a significant degree, has moved out of Sunday morning and out of church buildings into homes and the marketplace during the week.

An even greater difference, however, is that a hundred years ago the vast majority of the people engaged in continuing Bible study classes in the United States were in groups organized by leaders in the Sunday school movement or oldline denominations (Methodist, Baptist, Lutheran, Episcopal, Congregationalists, Disciples of Christ, Presbyterians, et al.). Today a large proportion of the people involved in adult Bible study classes are meeting in groups organized by parachurch agencies or by people from an organization not related to any denomination or local church or by leaders from a denomination that came into existence after the turn of the century.

A third difference between the Bible study programs of today and of thirty or sixty or ninety years ago is in the approach. Today dozens of different approaches are being used in the study of Scripture and some of the differences are so great, they are highly divisive. These divisions are often repeated within families or congregations or denominations and frequently are very destructive. It is possible, however, for some of these different approaches to be mutually reinforcing and enlightening.

This is one of the distinctive contributions made by Dick Murray in this book. He explains in detail a variety of approaches and suggests why and how a good teacher can be more effective by combining several approaches.

A fourth difference between today and yesteryear in regard to Bible study is the tremendous variety of pedagogical aids available to today's teacher. For generations individuals have been writing books on varying interpretations of the Scriptures. In recent decades, however, many more resources have become available both in the form of curriculum materials and in pedagogical concepts and ideas for teachers.

A major contribution of the author of this volume is a review of several different Bible study programs and of many pedagogical approaches.

Most of the widely used approaches to Bible study have followed one of two tracks. One has been to focus primarily on teaching people about the Bible. A second has been to help people become personally involved in what the Scriptures say to them in their religious pilgrimage. Dick Murray explains how both approaches can be brought together in one comprehensive approach.

The heart of this book, however, and the biggest contribution of the author, is Murray's insistence that an effective teacher uses a multifaceted approach that includes enthusiasm, witness, reflection, experience, and a love of God as well as emphasis on curriculum and pedagogical resources.

This is a book for the thoughtful, creative, reflective, and committed Christian who wants to share his or her faith with others through a systematic study of God's Holy Word.

LYLE E. SCHALLER
Yokefellow Institute
Richmond, Indiana

Contents

Contents

Preface

Once upon a time, many years ago, a group of eight persons met every Thursday evening for Bible study. They met in the living room of the parsonage, since they had no church building. The date was 1954, and the place was a small community in Northeast Texas called "Hooks."

The young pastor, only a few years out of seminary, was the leader. He sat with a copy of one volume of the *Interpreters' Bible* (a 12-volume commentary) on his lap while each member of the class worked out of the Bible translation of their choice.

The class spent an entire year, one-and-a-half hours a week, working their way through two books—I and II Thessalonians. The pastor had chosen to start with these books because they were two of Paul's earliest letters, and contained a sort of "Gospel according to Paul" possibly written before any of the Gospels themselves.

Each week the class worked through a portion of a chapter, verse by verse. Sometimes they spent the entire evening on only one verse.

Several housewives, two schoolteachers, a pawnbroker, an eighty-year-old minister's widow, and some workers in the nearby defense plant made up the group.

Everyone loved the class, was regular in attendance, was often puzzled by the "strange" understandings of others in the group, and felt that the experience contributed to the development of their faith.

This book springs from that class, and from four other primary sources:

First, my Bible teachers in seminary: James Muilenburg and Samuel Terrien in the Old Testament, John Knox and Frederick Grant in the New Testament. James Smart in biblical interpretation, and Bill Webber in a course on teaching methods for the Bible.

Second, the Bible classes I conducted during my years in local churches. Four faithful persons in Hyde Park, New York, several classes of ladies in trailer parks near Paducah, Kentucky, a group of dedicated teachers in Memphis, Tennessee, a great, open group of eight to ten in Hooks, Texas, a large class of sixty-five to eighty at First Methodist Church of Houston, Texas, who stayed with me for four years, and finally this year, a class in a new congregation in Estes Park, Colorado.

Third, my students and colleagues for twenty-one years at Perkins School of Theology. Hundreds of students have experimented with me in studying the Bible in class, and have visited, reported on, and given me permission to keep and use their reports. Bill Power, Jim Ward, Victor Furnish, Virgil Howard, John Holbert, and Bill Farmer, all first-rate biblical scholars, have helped me by frequent conversations and visits to my classes over the years, as have several other fellow teachers.

Fourth, three books have sparked my interest. *The Bible Speaks to You*, by Robert McAfee Brown, *The Unfolding Drama of the Bible*, by Bernhard Anderson, and *God's Unfolding Purpose*, by Suzanne de Dietrich, all came into my hands in the 1950s, and shaped my point of view, and my enthusiasm for Bible study.

As a seminary student I learned about the Bible. In the local church I learned the Bible itself. As a teacher I learned how to teach the Bible. In all of these I came to know God in a very personal fashion through encounter and dialogue with the text of the scripture, the life and teachings of Jesus Christ, and the enlivening of the Spirit. I yearn that each reader may have the privilege of such a journey and growth in the faith.

14

Research for this book has been aided by a grant from the Sam Taylor Fund, granted by the Section on Christian Education, General Board of Discipleship of the United Methodist Church, and by a study leave of one semester granted by Perkins School of Theology, Southern Methodist University.

Many pastors, Christian educators, and lay teachers have been interviewed by telephone or by personal visits, often accompanied by attendance at the Bible class they are currently teaching.

There is a revival of biblical teaching in the churches. This is especially true in metropolitan areas and their suburbs, and especially in the Midwest and South.

Finally, I am continually grateful to my wife, Joyce, who puts up with the commitment of time necessary for writing, and who has put the manuscript onto the word processor, patiently improving my spelling and grammar.

While I owe much to all these and others, I am, of course, solely responsible for the opinions and judgments of the contents.

DICK MURRAY
Estes Park, Colorado
Summer 1986

Introduction

You Are a Christian: The Bible Is Your Book

- ■ —Mainline Protestant churches are in trouble.
- ■ —Thousands now believe those churches are neglecting the Bible.
- ■ —Many people are turning elsewhere to do Bible study because—
- ■ —"Ignorance of the Scriptures is ignorance of Christ."
  —Jerome
- ■ —When our churches offer serious, interesting, and challenging Bible study, large numbers respond.
- ■ —This book is written to encourage and help pastors and laypersons to engage in life-changing Bible study.

Christians are a people of the Book. That book, the Bible, is the church's book. The church chose what to include, how to arrange the parts, and what to leave out. We, you and I, are the church, and the Bible, the church's book, is our book.

The Bible is our book because of what we believe that book reveals, a living God whom we know in Jesus Christ. We believe Jesus Christ is the living Word of God, and we must know the Bible if we are to know that living Word.

Unfortunately, for many Christians, that book has only been opened a tiny crack, and they are only vaguely aware of what is in and behind its pages. While there are likely to be one or more copies of the Bible in the homes of most Christians, it is their book in a technical sense only. For too many the Bible is but an object of vague veneration, rarely read or studied. This must mean that they are denied the full power of the living Christ revealed in the Bible, and therefore do not know God as they should.

For other Christians, the Bible is the great divider. When one of their children marries into a religious denomination other than their own, many parents discover that peace in the family depends on never discussing the Bible seriously again. Over the years, Christians have come to hate and mistrust, and even kill one another, over the different ways they have understood and interpreted the Bible.

In the 1980s in the United States and many other countries, this is precisely the case. The Bible is being used as an authority to determine and undergird political and social decisions and positions that are dividing churches, denominations, families, and the nation itself.

This is one reason for *The Strange Silence of the Bible in the Church*, the title of a book by James Smart, which though written many years ago, has been reprinted because it still speaks to our condition.

Some pastors have hesitated to teach Bible classes because they were afraid that such classes would reveal major differences within the congregation, or between them and the congregation. Many adult Sunday school classes avoid too much discussion of the Bible, because they have seen what the differences thus revealed have done to destroy other classes. Far too many of our youth are functionally illiterate in regard to the Bible and feel "dumb" when youth from other churches quote Bible passages to them, in order to prove a point.

Nevertheless, there has been and is a major new interest in Bible study in mainline churches, Protestant and Roman Catholic. This new interest springs from a variety of sources that have co-mingled to prompt the change.

The Second Vatican Council has not only influenced Roman Catholicism in regard to Bible study, but also Protestants. A new interest in following a lectionary of scripture readings in worship and preaching has been a factor, as has been a new emphasis on biblical preaching itself.

The proliferation of television evangelists, who are seen daily by millions, and who quote the Bible as the authority for their beliefs and actions, has prompted Christians of other points of view to turn back to their understanding of the Bible.

Possibly more than any other factor has been the growth of popular independent Bible study groups and programs. Sometimes led by charismatic-type personalities, such groups have attracted many members of mainline churches who felt they were not being offered similar or adequate Bible study opportunities in their own churches.

A considerable number of these groups represent the evangelical emphasis of our churches, and serve to remind all of us that we have neglected the Bible to a far greater degree than we have realized.

The response of both Protestant and Roman Catholic churches has been to introduce a wide variety of new curriculum resources for Bible study. In several denominations there is an infinite variety from which to choose. In addition, there are many fine independent studies that are now available for almost any taste or interest. Some of these will be described in this book.

Unfortunately the growth of Bible study curriculum resources has not been matched by a similar growth in the training of teachers to teach the Bible. Today's shortage of the Bible is not in the curricula, but in the teachers!

We, the teachers (lay and clergy), are the ones who need to have more Bible within us, and who need to try to involve others by more interesting, creative, and imaginative approaches to Bible study.

This book is written with three major convictions:

1. The Bible is the primary written revealer of God through Jesus Christ, and study of the Bible can reveal God better than any other source.

But the content of the Bible must always be transparent so the Christian can see the living God behind its cover and through every page.

The Bible was not written so the reader would know and love the Bible alone.

The Bible was written so the reader might know and love God.

2. It is possible (but not easy) to study the Bible from a variety of perspectives and positions of faith, and not come to mistrust those who disagree, *if* the ultimate knowledge sought is the love of God in Jesus Christ.

3. A vital key to achieving this goal is to balance *knowledge about* with *involvement with* both the texts of the Bible and the God of the Bible.

We believe the Bible spoke then and that it speaks now. We believe it spoke to them and that it speaks to us. Through Bible study, the church seeks to help persons become increasingly aware of God's seeking love as known especially in Jesus Christ and to respond in faith and love (a modification of an old definition of Christian education).

Deliberately not included here are several basic or classic scholarly approaches to Bible study. I have not included an approach using basic **introduction questions** such as: *Who* wrote it? *When* was it writen? *To whom* was it written? From *where* was it written? *Why* was it written? and, *What* does it contain? All of these questions are often included and dealt with in most of the approaches described but not as a separate approach in and of itself.

Nor have I laid out the details of standard exegetical analysis of a text. Commonly used as a first step by biblical scholars and careful preachers, this approach examines each word in the text along with other possible meanings and translations, and compares and questions the literary, historical, and cultural roots of the word. Here too, this approach will be used to some extent in several of the chapters, but not as a separate approach.

Ten Suggestions for Teaching the Bible to Adults and Youth

■— 1. Make the teaching of the Bible by the pastor and laypersons a priority in your church. Regular Bible study can be "leaven in the lump" of the life of the congregation.

■— 2. Remind yourself that we expect and depend on God's guidance in Bible study. We do not believe God will come if we ask, and stay away if we do not. Rather, we believe God is present in the Scriptures, in the lives of class members, in the world, and in ourselves. We teach the Bible in an attitude and atmosphere of prayer, without expecting or claiming that God will protect us from error, or make us correct in any interpretation.

■— 3. Offer a variety of Bible classes regularly, not just for a few weeks during Lent and Advent. Different members of the congregation will require a variety of approaches as their spiritual and intellectual needs change and mature.

■— 4. Organize Bible classes to be taught at several different times during the week, not just on Sunday morning, when time is quite restricted. Several valuable approaches to Bible study require an hour and a half or more.

■— 5. Insure that there are opportunities both to study the facts of the Bible and to be involved in caring Bible groups that get deeply involved with the Bible and with one another.

■— 6. Grin, cross your fingers, and find time and courage as the pastor to teach the Bible to youth yourself. Today's youth desperately need to feel themselves loved by the God of the Bible, as known especially in Jesus Christ. In their struggle with drugs, and alcohol, sex, money, and the search for a meaningful life, youth need to see that God has sustained many others in similar need.

■— 7. Although youth and adults can at times enjoy and benefit from being in the same Bible classes, youth can usually get more involved if they are in groups of their own. If youth are included in Bible classes with adults, they should be divided into subgroups of their own for questions and discussion; otherwise the youth will be overshadowed by more aggressive adults.

■— 8. Train teachers to use a rhythm between "standing outside the Bible looking in" (objectively) and "standing inside the Bible looking around" (subjectively). The two aspects need not and should not be equally balanced in every class, but the use of both can lead to new aspects of maturity and insight into the Bible.

■— 9. Enrich the weekly sermon's use of the Bible by combining it periodically with one or more of the approaches that involve the congregation in study of the same text before or after the sermon.

■—10. Avoid the church professionals' deadly disease of being so involved in the business of the church that you neglect the substance of the gospel in your own life. This applies to overcommitted laypersons as well.

Let teaching the Bible aid you in your move toward spiritual maturity.

PART I

YOU ARE A TEACHER OF THE BIBLE TO ADULTS OR YOUTH

Sunday School Teacher, Pastor, Christian Educator

You Teach the Bible with *Mind* and *Heart, Enthusiasm* and *Witness*

- —I have never met a Christian youth or adult who did not "want to want" to study the Bible.

- —There is a yearning to yearn, a feeling of need and incompleteness that is almost universal in the church.

- —Nevertheless, the vast majority do little Bible study.

- —Most Christian adults and youth are waiting for a good teacher—

    to motivate them
    to inspire them
    to involve them
    to interest them
    to inform them
    to love them

■—You can be that teacher!

The clue to your success is the combining of the *mind* and *heart*, thinking and feeling, within the compass of your own enthusiasm, and witness to your own faith. You need not be an accomplished Bible scholar, but you must be open to learning what others have discovered concerning the Scriptures, and you must be open to the quickening of the Spirit of God as you work your way along with a class.

Learning about God must be accompanied by finding God personally, and allowing God to find you. Youth and adults want their teachers to tell the truth concerning both their faith and their doubts. They want teachers to be both enthusiastic and candid, as they share their new insights and commitments.

In the next several sections you will find suggestions for making your teaching both effective and interesting. You will be familiar with some of these approaches, and others will be quite new. Some will appeal to you at once and others will turn you off, at least at the beginning.

Be courageous. Step out and experiment with some of these ideas and approaches. Tell your class you have never done this before, smile, and then go ahead and try what is suggested. Use your imagination to modify the approaches in order to adapt to the needs and interests of your class.

Your rewards will be—

Your own development as a Bible student.

The appreciation and enthusiasm of your class.

The deepening of the spiritual life of both you and your
    pupils.

1

You Teach "About" and You Get "Involved With" the Bible

- —Knowing the stories, ideas, and persons in the Bible is one important part of Bible study.
- —Getting emotionally and thoughtfully involved with the stories, ideas, and persons in the Bible is another important part of Bible study.
- —Moving back and forth between these two approaches is essential for the development of Christian faith.
- —"Apply yourself totally to the text:
  Apply the text totally to yourself."
  —J. A. Bengel, 1734

Many people spend much of their lives studying about the Bible, but never allow themselves to get involved with the Bible. They know a great deal about God, but have never gotten involved with God. Some Sunday school teachers rush through their material to be sure the lesson is covered, but never slow down enough to allow God to touch the lives of the participants.

Good teaching of the Bible is always a rhythm between learning about the Bible and getting involved with the Bible and the God of the Bible.

When the teacher says, "Jesus often taught in parables, of

which one of the most well known is called the 'Parable of the Prodigal Son,' " the teacher is telling the class *about* the Bible. We hear what is said and our minds say, That sounds interesting, tell me more.

But when the teacher begins, "Once upon a time a man had two sons, each of whom had very different outlooks on life," we are getting *involved with* the parable and the Bible. No longer are we standing outside the Bible looking in with interest at a person who told parables. We have now been moved by the teacher inside the Bible, where we are meeting people quite like ourselves.

When the teacher continues with, "One son took his share of the estate and wasted it, while the other son stayed at home and worked faithfully all his life," we are already choosing sides within our minds. We cannot keep from getting involved, because we have brothers who are like that, and we have strong feelings about such behavior.

That is the key word: *feelings*. We study about the Bible with our minds, we get involved with the Bible through both our minds and feelings.

Another example of the contrast between *about* and *involved with* is in the story of Abraham and Sarah in chapters 20 and 21 of Genesis. What *was* Sarah's relationship to Abraham? Wife? sister? half sister? In trying to answer this question you are trying to learn objectively *about*.

But when you ask, "How must Sarah have felt when she was offered to another man?" or, "How must Sarah have felt when she had a child in her old age?" you are very emotionally *involved with*.

Some teachers of the Bible think that "getting the class involved with the scripture" is the only important thing to do in Bible study, and these teachers never "bore their class with facts about the Bible." Such teachers seem to assume that only the personal opinions and feelings of the class are of any value, and the finds of biblical scholars are of little or no importance. This is as unbalanced as putting all one's emphasis on information and data from scholars with no involvement with the text of the Bible oneself.

Significant teaching of the Bible moves back and forth to some degree between objectively standing outside and subjectively getting inside the biblical text. This does not mean that a good teacher gives equal attention to these two facets in every lesson, but it does mean that teachers at one time or another realize the importance of both.

Nor does this imply that so-called lectures are always *about*, and that discussion is always *involved with* the Bible itself. Many verbal presentations or lectures use involvement techniques such as the telling of stories, while I have taken part in far too many so-called "discussions" about the Bible that were only an exchange of strongly held theological positions, with no involvement in the biblical text at all. (See chapter 2 on lecture and discussion.)

One of the best ways I know to illustrate what I mean by "About" and "Involved With" is a method of Bible study that includes both, and one that I have used for many years. It can be used with families, older children, young people, or adults. They will all enjoy and benefit from it. For want of a better title, I call it:

Identification of and Identification with Bible Stories Through Pictures.

Using biblical pictures that contain clues to which biblical story the picture portrays, this method of Bible teaching moves from correct identification of the picture and the story to the sharing of one's personal thoughts and feelings concerning the persons, events, or occasion portrayed.

Thus, if you have a picture that shows a man holding two stone tablets with Hebrew writing on them, you can probably assume that this is Moses with the Ten Commandments.

This is the first step in identification "of." This part is enriched if the members of the class recall as much of the story as they can and the teacher supplies additional details.

Part 2 of this approach is to share in a small group what the story of the giving of the Ten Commandments has meant in your life. This sharing can be very enriching and spiritually stimulating.

PROCEDURE

1. Collect a group of such pictures from old Sunday school packets or other sources. (Look in closets for children's material of several years ago.)

Be sure the pictures you use contain hints or clues to the incident that will enable a knowledgeable person to correctly identify them. Some appropriate pictures would be:

> Moses and the Burning Bush
> Ruth and Naomi
> Joseph and His Coat of Many Colors
> Jeremiah Wearing a Yoke Around His Neck
> Jesus in the Temple As a Boy
> Jesus and His Disciples in a Boat

It is always more interesting if some of the identifications are quite difficult.

(One very fine set of Old Testament pictures published several years ago was entitled "In His Image," painted by Guy Rowe and published by Oxford University Press. Although no longer in print, many of these sets can still be found.)

2. Number the pictures and place them on a table in front of the class. Give everyone a pencil and piece of paper, and ask them to circulate the pictures, writing down their identifications. (You may want to suggest that persons work in pairs to aid self-confidence.)

3. After an adequate time, have the class go back to their seats and go through the pictures, asking for the correct identification of each picture. (Let every person keep his or her own score.)

After each picture has been identified, ask someone to tell the story that that picture represents. Others may add to the story, and you may want to supplement what is said.

Do Not hurry. Take plenty of time to think about each picture.

When all the pictures have been identified, you may want to see who has the best score without embarrassing those who did poorly.

Obviously this first exercise is *about* the Bible. For each picture there is a correct answer.

Does such study deepen and enlarge Christian faith? This type of exercise may simply build the ego and pride of those who do well, and cause others to feel inferior. Such knowledge of the basic stories of the Bible, however, can open new possibilities for meeting personally the God of the Bible.

Several of the most popular series of Bible study today, such as *Bethel* and *Trinity*, put a great deal of emphasis on *knowing* such information.

4. At this point, this approach seeks to help these stories of the Bible to become your story.

Ask the class members to look at all the pictures again and ask each member to choose one picture with which he or she can personally identify in some way. Be sure to include some pictures of women.

This identification might be—

A childhood interest in the story such as Joseph and his brothers.

A personal and persistent challenge from Jeremiah wearing a yoke.

A persistent tug from a story such as Jesus calling his disciples.

The teacher may want to model such involvement by sharing his or her thoughts and feelings concerning one of the pictures.

5. Divide the class into groups of three or four and ask group members one at a time to share their "involvement with" one of the stories. Suggest that the other members of the group be active listeners, helping the teller to explore his or her feelings and thoughts, but they are not in any way to try to "correct" the personal sharing. Here, of course, there is no correct or incorrect data—simply interesting personal involvement with the biblical story.

Allow at least five minutes for each person to share—possibly a good deal more.

It would rarely be helpful or appropriate to ask for each group to share its discussion. It would take too much time, and such secondhand sharing of deep feelings or ideas can rarely be done well in a larger group.

Allow from an hour and a half to two hours for this approach.

Note the different contribution of both types of activities. When we study *about* the Bible we are laying the base for getting *involved with* the Bible.

Over the long term, our knowledge about gradually informs our involvement with the biblical text. Such knowledge sometimes corrects and at times confuses our involvement with the text, but the balance is always needed.

The theme of this book is that both *about* and *involved with* Bible study are needed to deepen and enlarge our Christian faith, the real goal of Bible study.

2

You Teach Through Lectures and Discussion

■ —Teaching may be defined as stimulating and enabling

Involvement
with
Information
to influence
Results

■ —Teaching the Bible in the church places that process within brackets of trust in God.

■ —Thus, a Bible class outline includes:
Trust—Involvement—Information—Results—Trust.

■ —When you are talking (lecturing), you and the class should be:
Thinking, Feeling, Deciding

■ —When the class is talking (discussing), you and the class should be:
Thinking, Feeling, Deciding

■ —You should usually include both.

This is not a book about teaching methods, but methods are the tools all teachers use to carry out any of the many approaches described and illustrated in the following chapters. Therefore, a few thoughts concerning methods, and what we want them to do:

What are some contributions of lectures and discussion?

Every Good Bible Class
(of 30 minutes or 2½ hours)
Should Include:

Trust

You and the class believe and trust that God is present and active in your class. You believe God is present and active in each person in the group, in the Scriptures, and in the fellowship of the church. You may acknowledge and point to that presence by offering prayer at the beginning of the class, or you may not, but all believe God is there, and that God's presence is important.

Involvement

Many people believe this means discussion, but that is only partially the case. Involvement is not in the mouth, involvement is in the mind. A participant is involved when he or she is thinking, feeling, and deciding about the information at hand, whether or not he or she ever says anything.

A teacher can involve people at a very high level when giving a very stimulating, thought-provoking lecture. A teacher can also involve the class by using procedures that engage everyone in small group discussion.

Discussion

The keys to successful discussion are *group size* and *group assignment*.

When listening to a lecture, most class members do not expect to talk (unless to ask questions). When in a group discussion, most class members (not all) do expect to talk. Therefore, discussion groups should be divided according to the amount of time available, subject to be discussed, amount of desired emotional involvement, discussion assignment, and expected results.

The fastest and easiest groups are pairs, which are easy to form, even in pews. Say, "Nudge your neighbor and talk about _____." Groups of three can also be organized easily anywhere, without moving chairs. The larger the small groups, the longer it takes for many in the group to share.

For youth, groups need to avoid embarrassment, with detailed, specific assignments. Adults often appreciate such assignments too.

Check to be sure the assignments are understood by all.

Groups do not need to report (on what was said or decided), but they may want to share some of their key ideas.

Information

Some information is "hard" factual data. Other information is "soft"—such as opinions, feelings, and attitudes—which are of course factual in their own way.

Such information can be told, read by each person, viewed and heard on video, or it can be generated in serious discussion. In whatever way information comes, the persons in Bible classes want to know. Ignorance is not bliss.

Lectures

Lectures may be as long as one hour (very long!) or as short as five minutes. Whatever their length, they should concentrate on doing things for that class which that class would find difficult to do for themselves.

In listening to, and appreciating, the lectures of great Bible scholars, I have often been helped most by their telling the group the questions they ask of the biblical text. Then I have thought, How could I be so dense? I had never thought of that.

I also like to go to hear biblical lecturers who tell the Bible stories in interesting, imaginative ways. All lecturers need to learn to be good storytellers, looking for different ways to stimulate the imagination of their listeners.

Bible lecturers are also helpful when they provide information from beyond the reading of the average class member, or when they share the opinions and judgments of a variety of points of view.

Good lecturers frequently use the expressions: Did you know? Have you heard? Have you ever thought? It seems to me." "As I read." "As I reflected." A good lecturer has something to say, says it clearly, in an interesting fashion, and does not say too much.

(For additional suggestions on lectures and discussion, see my book *Strengthening the Adult Sunday School Class*, Abingdon, 1981.)

Results

Results may be small or large, but we always hope to influence them. Notice, I did not say "force" or "create" them. Results may include new knowledge, new insight, new inspiration, new feelings, new attitudes, new visions, or new choices. In fact, the results may not be actually all that "new," but only slight modifications or adaptations of what already exists.

Trust

As you started the class, by trusting that God is present and active in the participants, in the Scriptures, and in the group, so you end the class, with that same trust. You do not finish the class, you simply stop, for now, and trust that in the end—God.

3

You Use Depth Bible Study

- ■ —This approach digs deeper and deeper to personal involvement.
- ■ —What do we need to know *about* this text?
- ■ —What did the author have in mind then for them?
- ■ —What does the text mean to us—now?

This is the most basic approach to Bible study and teaching. Every preacher asks questions like those above in preparing for a sermon. Most Sunday school materials are organized to progress in this way.

The entire process can be done by one person in a lecture or sermon, but it is far better Bible study if the entire class is involved by being divided into small groups.

Ross Snyder, a well-known Christian educator, once described this approach as like peeling the layers of an onion. The closer you get to the center, the more you are personally involved. In fact, you can end up in tears!

Depth Bible study seeks to move from the informational level of Bible study to a confrontational level, where the individual feels personally involved. It is used in a wide variety of ways, but there is always some use of both objective information and subjective opinion. The ultimate goal is always to get to the heart of the matter—God and yourself.

In many ways my use of this method over the last thirty years (beginning in 1954) is responsible for the rationale of this book in seeking a rhythm between "about" and "involvement with" in good Bible study.

Such Bible study assumes that the scripture had both meaning in its own time and meaning in our time. This meaning may be nearly the same, then and now, or it may be quite different, depending on changes in circumstances and understanding. At any rate, neither is irrelevant to the other.

PROCEDURE

1. When possible, a portion of Scripture should be assigned in advance, as for example Matthew 20:1-16, usually called the "Parable of the Laborers." Participants should be asked to try to read it as if for the first time, looking for new insights, particular problems, or questions they had not thought of before.

This first reading can be done either at home in advance, or in class after persons arrive.

There may be a general sharing of insights and questions in preparation for the second set of questions.

Since these are personal insights, they are really not arguable, but should be heard with interest by all. The object is to put on "freshener glasses," and to search for new personal insights.

2. What does this text actually say? This is always the starting point. Try to let the text speak for itself. What happens in this story as Jesus tells it? Be sure you have the story straight. Then ask, What do you think Jesus intended to convey when he told this parable? What did this parable likely mean to its first hearers?

In responding to these questions, your class should work in pairs or threes, first asking these questions of themselves. After a few minutes, additional information should be introduced to the class from the writings of various Bible scholars.

Two or three class members could have been assigned to read commentaries, and to report, or the teacher may supply that information. (If there were plenty of time, all could use such resources on their own.)

Warning: There will often be a tendency to quickly "modernize" the passage and not allow it to be understood in its own time and setting. There may also be persons who have a strongly held opinion of the passage's meaning, which they wish to impose on the group. Both tendencies should be resisted.

Of course, different commentaries may vary in their information, so these differences will need to be acknowledged.

Depending on scripture used, other sub-questions in this section might include—

—What did the author wish to say for God?
—What seems to be the central idea or purpose?

I am sure it is obvious that neither scholars nor your class can be sure of their answers, because that information is simply not available.

In regard to Matthew 20:1-16, most commentators will stress that Jesus is speaking of God and the kingdom of Heaven. He is not speaking of labor relations, even in his own day, much less in ours. He is telling the parable to Jews in a Jewish setting. Jesus is speaking about righteousness, which Jews believed came from adherence to God's law. Jesus says this is not the criterion for the kingdom of Heaven—God's grace is a gift—not earned, but given. God

37

bestows grace wherever He wills, which may appear to be unfair to those who have carefully kept the law.

Step 2 has thus been an attempt to be as objective as possible, to stand outside the passage while looking at it, and to ask questions for facts whenever possible.

In steps 3 and 4, we turn more personal and toward the present. We add our feelings to ideas, and we subjectively try to bring the passages into our own lives.

3. What meaning does this passage have for us today?

In view of our situation in the late twentieth century, what does this passage say to us? What elements are the same or different in the situation then and now? What does this mean for the church in contrast to Jews in Jesus' time?

I have found that a few minutes for each person to work alone with pencil and paper will often enhance his or her discussion in 2s or 3s a few minutes later.

Sharing from the subgroups may focus around questions like, What were one or two of the most interesting responses in your group? or, What was a major problem for your group?

At this point, the teacher may want to share additional points of view of his or her own, or suggest other opinions that have not been expressed by the group, possibly quite different from theirs.

4. What is the meaning of the passage for you? How do you feel about what it says or implies? If I took this passage seriously, would I have to make changes in my life?

At this point, it is important for all to think and work alone and to share verbally only if they feel free to do so.

It is often appropriate for the teacher to model possible responses and to summarize and draw the study to a close. The teacher should never force or push personal sharing.

A prayer of thanksgiving and the seeking of God's

strength and help is a good way to end. Several members of the class may wish to share verbally in this prayer.

To use this method as outlined with much group participation requires from an hour to an hour and a half. If the teacher supplies much of the data and ideas, the time can be considerably shorter.

Young people can and will participate fully in this approach, but they will need to be encouraged frequently by careful and patient directions and examples.

This approach combines information "about" and "involvement with" quite well. It moves beyond many Sunday school lessons, both in interest in data, and in personal commitment. In a real sense, "the word can become flesh" in the lives of those using this approach, and participants can respond with deep commitment.

4

You Use Theological Bible Study

- ■ —The God questions.

- ■ —The person questions.

- ■ —The relationship questions.
        These are the basic questions of life.

- ■ —The Bible was written to address these very questions.

- ■ —These are all theological questions, because

- ■ —Theology means thinking and talking about God and all that God does.

- ■ —Asking theological questions of passages of Scripture often illuminates the Bible and gives us vital insights.

Professor W. J. A. Power, who teaches Old Testament at Perkins School of Theology in Dallas, Texas, first introduced me to the idea of calling this approach "Theological" Bible study. He found that in studying the early Hebrew narratives, especially in the book of Genesis, the most helpful questions in unlocking their fundamental meaning were theological. They were the God questions, the human questions, and the relationship questions resulting in the asking of the What must I do? question.

I have come to believe this approach is one of the most helpful ways to study the Bible.

AN EXAMPLE OF THIS APPROACH

About a year ago a group of us in a small church in Colorado were studying the passage in Exodus 3 concerning Moses and God at the burning bush in Midian.

Although we could easily have struggled with questions like, What did Moses *actually see?* or Did Moses *actually* "hear" God's voice with his ear or with his mind? accurate answers to either of these questions are of course impossible, and furthermore, whatever our answers, they would distress and even anger some Christians, who would disagree.

Instead, we concentrated that evening on the God—human—relationship questions, with interesting results. Individually, and then sharing in groups of four, we asked:

What does this passage tell us about God?
What does this passage tell us about men and women?
What does this passage tell us about the relationship between God and human beings?

After sharing in our groups, we compiled three lists on the chalkboard, in regard to the three questions. There was general surprise at how much this brief passage said, or implied, about each of the questions. In regard to God, we agreed that—

God seeks and gains contact with humans.
God, in fact, communicates with men and women.
God revealed Himself to Moses. But,
God was also mysteriously hidden from Moses.
God is dynamic and active.
God is concerned about the plight of His people.

Turning to the second question, we found that Moses as a representative person—

41

—"heard" God.

—was uncertain and frightened.

—felt compelled to respond to God.

—argued with God.

—stumbled along in responding to God, often wanting to turn back.

—was never quite sure he was doing the right thing.

Many persons in our small class identified with Moses and said, "How true of me!"

When we looked at what this passage says or emphasizes about the relationship between God and His creatures (as represented by Moses and the early Hebrews), we found that—

God initiates relationships with men and women, whether they like it or not.

God wants relationships with us, and goes to great efforts to establish them.

God is concerned about the plight of suffering people, and tries to lead human beings into ways to alleviate their problems.

Men and women are often distressed by the things they feel God wants, and resist God's obvious desires.

As our study group completed an hour and a half of work on this passage, there was general agreement among group members that they had come to realize a great deal about not only the early Hebrew relationship with God, but had also gained an amazing amount of insight concerning their own understanding of the God–person–relationship.

ANOTHER EXAMPLE

With another Bible class we used these same theological questions to probe a familiar New Testament passage,

I Corinthians 13. Almost everyone in the class had studied and even memorized much of this text as a child, and it felt like an old friend as we read it silently to ourselves.

Nevertheless, when our small groups began to ask the questions concerning God, human beings, and the relationship between them, familiar "ruts" in our minds concerning the supremacy of love were erased, and we moved into new areas of understanding.

The emphasis shifted from our behavior alone, to the enabling power of God, and we found ourselves moving into a new understanding of Paul's relationship with God—through His Lord, Jesus Christ.

The teacher raised more explicit "God questions," such as—

What does this passage tell us about God's love? God's forgiveness? God's patience?

Two Tendencies

In both classes described, we found the class drifting into one or the other of these tendencies:

On the one hand there was a tendency to harmonize everything that was said, thereby losing the very real differences in perspectives that had been "discovered" and shared by different persons. On the other hand was a tendency to push for one perspective as the "right" understanding, and to discard all others.

The teacher needed to carefully call attention to, often magnify and delineate, and insist on the right of even slight variations to stand on their own as helpful insights for all in the group.

As has been said before, "The greatest gift I have to give you is my difference from you."

SUMMARY

The Bible is a theological book written and preserved by the church to sustain and enhance faith by saying particular kinds of things about God, about men and women, about the world, and about the church.

This approach uses explicit and fundamental theological questions as the framework for study.

In a winter 1984 article in the *Perkins Journal*, Dr. Power, referring especially to the stories in the book of Genesis, says:

There are many kinds of questions that one might address to these stories. One could ransack them for their historical allusions; or one could try to uncover the social and economic settings from which they come, or one could try to ascertain the religious milieu which produced them. Each of these areas provides a valid range of questions that can lead to profitable and interesting study. But my concern here is to remind the reader that whatever other matters may be of interest to him, he ought never to forget that the Church comes to him with the claim that these stories are indeed "Word of God"; that they in fact do tell us the very truth about God's nature, where we stand in relationship to him, and something of what our common task is. (Vol. XXXVII, no. 2, p. 4)

There are, of course, many other theological questions concerning the church, sin, forgiveness, grave, revelation, and other important concepts that can be included when appropriate.

5

You Use Shared Praxis Bible Study

First, two definitions:

■ —"Shared"—Talking and listening together in a group.

■ —*"Praxis"* (a Greek word)—meaning that theory (thinking about) and practice (doing) are essentially interwoven. (There is no need to say this word ever again—unless you want to impress your class!)

Now, the emphasis:

■ —What we are now doing and thinking is where we begin learning (our stories).

■ —We need to know how the scripture has been understood, explained, and responded to by the church (*the* Story).

■ —Thinking and feeling about the interaction between our stories and the Story leads to,

■ —A new vision and hope born from our lives in dialogue with the Bible.

In many Sunday school classes for adults or youth that I have visited, this is what I have observed:

A. 1. The scripture is read.
   2. The teacher tells what the quarterly says, or has the class read what it says.
   3. The teacher then gives her or his opinion.
   4. The teacher asks the opinions of the class, and what they think they ought to do.

Or

B. 1. The scripture is read.
   2. The teacher asks the participants how they respond to the scripture.
   3. The teacher tells what the quarterly says about the biblical text.
   4. The teacher asks, "Well, what does this mean we should be, or do?"

Shared *praxis* is actually an improved form of "B." Thomas Groome, a fine Roman Catholic Christian educator, has given this approach an interesting name and a greatly strengthened structure. This is my understanding, in brief, of Groome's Shared Praxis:

The scripture is read. The teacher then leads the class in five steps, or movements, possibly asking first:

1. What do you hear or feel?
2. Think about what your hear. Why do you and others in the class hear or feel that?
3. What are the major things the scholars, and the church, have said about this scripture?
4. Think about what the commentaries have said in interaction with what you have heard and felt.
5. Look at the vision of the scripture and choose a vision of your own.

A MODEL FOR USING SHARED PRAXIS IN BIBLE STUDY

Matthew 6:25-34; Luke 12:22-34, commonly called "Words of Jesus on Anxiety."
Read Matthew 6:25-34. If Bibles are available, or if scripture is printed in the Sunday school material, the class

can read aloud, slowly, in unison. (Be sure not to embarrass any poor reader in your class.)

Summary of scripture: Jesus begins, "Therefore I tell you, do not be anxious about your life," and he goes on to talk about how God has taken care of even birds and flowers, and He will surely take care of us, His human children. Jesus says we should "seek first his kingdom and his righteousness, and all these things shall be yours as well."

1. Using Shared Praxis, the teacher then asks a question like, What is the primary message you hear from this passage? The emphasis is on personal response, not correct ideas. (If the class is very large, you may want to ask them to discuss the questions in pairs or trios, and then hear from several such groups.)

2. The teacher then leads the class to think and reflect on their responses. Questions for this lesson might be: Has this passage ever concerned you? How have you felt? What causes anxiety in you? Have you ever been in great physical need? How did you feel? What is the difference between concern and anxiety?

3. The teacher or some other well-informed person now either tells the class or leads the class to read the major things scholars and the commentaries say about the significance and meaning of this portion of Scripture. (This may come largely from the Sunday school material.)

The information might include:

The KJV translation "takes no thought," although this is misleading, and the RSV is better when it says, "Do not be anxious." The emphasis of Jesus seems to be clearly on basic

47

trust in God (transcending all anxieties) and the call to men and women to keep the coming kingdom as their primary goal.

Nevertheless, some Christians have interpreted this passage to suggest a passive dependence on God, one in which you should not work hard to support yourself, but should instead trust that God will provide all you need. These Christians believe it their duty to pray with great confidence that despite the circumstances, everything they need will appear.

The church, by and large, has rejected this latter interpretation.

In this presentation, the teacher offers this information in an open and nonauthoritative way, making it clear that this data does not need to be accepted at face value, with no modification or change.

4. The teacher now asks the class to think about both what they have just heard about Scripture (the Story) and their own earlier responses to the passage. Each person is asked to look for contrasts, meeting points, and confrontations.

The teacher asks, What insights did the information on the passage provide for you? What would you add to or wish to clarify? Are there contrasts between your original response and what the material has said? Are you encouraged by any aspects of the information?

Are some personalities more prone genetically or culturally to have anxieties than others? Does this mean these persons have less faith in God? Reflect on the relationship between concern for daily needs and trust in God.

5. Finally, the teacher leads the class to make a "faith response" to the future. The class is led into thinking and feeling about the vision and hope that seems to arise from,

and is called for, by the interaction of the participants and the scripture.

The questions for this lesson might be: How will these reflections influence how you deal with your anxieties in the future? Does this scripture point to a hope and vision that gives you a new hope for yourself? Do you want to decide in your own mind what you will choose to do?

Some pastors and teachers may ask, How is this any different from what we have been doing all along? For a few, there may be little difference, but for most of us, two or three important elements or emphases have been added.

1. The emphasis on asking probing, insightful questions, especially in steps 2 and 4. In my experience most teachers have neglected to practice and learn the art of leading this vital aspect of reflective thinking.

2. Offering the wisdom of scholars and the church at large in an open, dialogical manner, which does not imply that this is the last and final insight, and at the same time, paying careful attention to it.

3. Working hard in the entire process to include both *thought* and *feeling,* and to keep both actual practice and ideas about practice together in one whole (praxis).

The key to success in using this approach is the skill of asking questions. Questions that help participants search—search within their own minds, memories, and experience. Questions that lead the class to search within their feelings, hurts, and joys. Questions that search within the scripture, searching within the statements of experts, searching within the history and traditions of the church.

Questions that search the divine.

Groome does not insist that these steps be done rigidly in this order, and many teachers will adapt them in a variety of ways. I have tried using this approach in this order: Steps 3, and then 1, 2, 4, and 5.

You will note that although this approach starts at a very different point then depth Bible study, both go through much the same process, and end on a similar note. Thee two approaches will probably be regularly useful by teachers of youth and adults.

When using Shared Praxis with youth, the teacher will want to be creative in involving them actively at every possible point. Steps 1 and 2 can be expressed in a variety of creative ways, and step 3 can be done through group research of available material.

Shared Praxis can be used in a wide variety of time spans. Since discussion is an essential part of the process, and since the larger the class the more time discussion takes, the size of your group has a lot to do with the time required. Basically, I believe the process can be done in forty to fifty minutes, although I would prefer an hour and a half.

Those who want to know far more about shared praxis should read *Christian Religious Education* (Thomas H. Groome, New York: Harper and Row, Publishers, 1980).

6

You Use Dialogue and Encounter

■ —The three basic dialogues in life are:

Between me and myself
Between me and my neighbor
Between me and God.

■ —We bring these dialogues to the Bible, and we find these same dialogues in the Bible.

■ —Dialogue is the basis of all relationships. When dialogue stops, relationships erode.

■ —In dialogue we are encountered, confronted, and challenged by ourselves, others, and God.

■ —Much scripture demands dialogue and forces encounter: mentally, emotionally, and spiritually.

Fred Gealy, a rare person who taught both the New Testament and church music at Perkins School of Theology, and later at the Methodist Theological School in Ohio, died in 1976. For many of us who knew him, he also taught a firm and yet gentle kind of servanthood, as he cared for many years for the daily needs of his invalid wife.

Gealy described and used a type of Bible study also used by many others. This is described in a brief article entitled, "Dialogue and Encounter: An Approach to the Scriptures," printed in 1960 as "Monograph 1" by The Austin Experiment of the Christian Faith and Life Community, Austin, Texas.

In many ways this is a combination of the basic approach

of Depth Bible study and Theological Bible study, often including elements of the use of all the senses in approaching the text of the scripture.

The helpfulness of this approach is closely tied to the mature discovery of Professor Gealy, the biblical scholar, and Fred Gealy, the searching Christian, that while historical-critical analysis must be pursued seriously and carefully, it cannot, in and of itself, unlock the mysteries of the revelations of a living God.

Gealy says,

The power of the Bible over us is due to a very great extent to the fact that from beginning to end it is made up of dialogues which reach out and inescapably involve us. Paradoxically enough, the dialogues are *in us* before they are in the Bible. These dialogues which are in us and in which we are, are always three directional:
Between me and myself
Between me and my neighbor
Between me and God.

Gealy goes on, "Only as we keep it [i.e., the dialogue] open, only as we can increase and not decrease the significant encounter areas of life and thereby maintain the dialogue, can we understand either the Bible, or the Christian faith, or life itself" (p. 4).

Gealy believed that far too many people try to find absolute answers in the Bible, rather than continuing, every day of their lives, to look for a living God who wants and insists on combining encounter and dialogue.

GEALY'S PRINCIPLES OF DIALOGUE

Dialogue must never be allowed to end by an absolute answer or resolution. There is always something to probe further, if not today, then tomorrow.

Within myself—The hidden subtleties and contradictions of the human mind, emotions, and spirit.

With my neighbor—The incredible discoveries of our different perceptions and feelings, and the sources and reinforcements behind them.

With God—The constant tension between a God who is so close and intimate, and is yet so distant and different from ourselves, who is very "other," and confronts us with agonizing and incomprehensible pain.

Thus, every question is not followed by an answer but rather by another question.

GEALY'S PRINCIPLES OF INTERPRETATION

The Bible was written for thelogical reasons—to deal with theological questions, and therefore must always be interpreted theologically.

Rationalistic interpretations, using scientific or psychological reasoning, must always be rejected as too neat and easy.

Literalistic interpretations must likewise be set aside in any doubtful or complicated situation, because they also shut off any possibility of future dialogue.

The interpreter must sit before the text and ask theological questions concerning the text's witness to God, to human beings, and to the broken and healed relationship between God and ourselves.

As an example, look at the story of Jesus walking on the water in John 6:16–21. The theological approach says that while the human mind of the twentieth century demands that we ask, What actually happened? we must always know that an answer to that question is usually quite irrelevant to understanding the text. The literalist may say it is obvious that Jesus did just that—walked on the water.

The rationalist may say that it is obvious human bodies do not walk on water—they sink—and therefore there is another and rational explanation.

Gealy would insist neither of these points of view is helpful, because both want and insist on ending the dialogue. Rather, the reader must probe with mind, emotions, and spirit the theological reasoning of the writer, his or her own theological understanding, and ultimately the revelation of God, which lives in, behind, and through the text.

Thus, this story in the gospel of John is intended to record a miracle. You do not explain away a miracle, or it would no longer be a miracle. You allow a miracle to stand as a mysterious record, and you ask:

What did this miracle mean to them?
What does this miracle mean to us? and finally,
What does God have to say to us in this miracle record?

In this particular scripture, Gealy points out that it is quite clear that this Jesus, whom the disciples called "Lord," is certainly also the "Lord of the sea," and is our Lord as well.

This understanding of scripture has a theological and spiritual meaning, which continues to unfold and is never absolute or closed.

This approach also insists that we talk too much about our finding God in the Bible, and do not realize that it is often God who finds us in the Scripture. In fact, if we get deeply into many passages of Scripture we realize that God is relentlessly pursuing us, and we simply cannot escape. God has us by the foot, and we are caught! In fact, at times God asks us so many questions as we study the text that we can hardly get in any questions of our own.

The reader will realize that I have described the rationale of this approach in far more detail than that of other approaches. I have done so because I believe the rationale is the major contribution of this approach, and also because I personally find this approach to be very close to the way I need to study the Bible as I near my retirement. Many neat answers of my youth no longer suffice to enrich and deepen my faith.

POSSIBLE PROCEDURE

Fred Gealy never prescribed a procedure for this approach. He usually led this kind of study through a combination of "Dialogical-Monologue," in which he would musingly ask questions, and then work on the answers himself, as well as ask probing Socratic-type questions of the class. Gealy was always seeking great mental participation, and he never allowed a response to stand without an additional question, some modification from him, or turning to someone else for an additional response from a somewhat different perspective. The class often turned into a hard-driving, mind-stimulating, emotion-stirring dialogue.

Nevertheless, many of us are not accomplished enough *as* either lecturers or questioners to use this style well.

ANOTHER PROCEDURE

1. Prepare carefully by studying the text, reading all available commentaries, and thinking and praying about the deep possibilities.

2. Assign participants to do the same, in advance if possible.

3. Outline the rationale of this approach to the class, or if you have used it frequently, remind them of the key points.

4. Divide the class into work groups of three or four persons.

5. Ask the groups to discuss:

—What does the writer intend to say? What does this text intend to communicate? What does it say?

—If the text includes an event: What actually happened? What were the primary impulses in the original event? What really occurred?

Ask the groups to work ten to twenty minutes on these questions, utilizing the reading they have done in advance, and listening to the findings and insights of the others in their group.

6. Have some sharing from the groups, probe and add to the responses, push for other points of view and thought. They are, of course, intended to be "about" questions that are responded to as objectively as possible. (It would be quite appropriate, and often helpful, to use chapter 8, "Spectrum Bible Study," at this point in the process.)

7. Have the work groups move on to:

—What do I say? As twentieth-century people what do we say to this kind of text?

—What does God say to me? How am I involved in this situation? What claims does this passage place on me?

8. After fifteen to twenty minutes in the groups, invite some sharing in which you, as leader, both listen and challenge, both affirm and probe. Keep the dialogue open and continuing.

9. Add additional information on your own, and share your own insights and feelings, all the while inviting responses from the class.

10. Look for, pull out, and examine theological insights and spiritual implications of the passage.

The teacher will see that this approach requires hard work, considerable risk, emotional commitment, and spiritual growth. There are also major rewards.

7

You Use All the Senses in Bible Study

■ —Thought is only one of God's gifts to us.

■ —"In Bible Study the absence of emotion is ignorance."
—John Holbert

■ —Seeing, hearing, touching, smelling, and tasting all help us to think and react emotionally. All communicate to us.

■ —Deep personal, intellectual, and emotional involvement in the substance of the scripture can be life-changing—even transforming.

I am going to introduce and illustrate here two variations on the use of the senses and imagination (as well as the mind), hopefully resulting in major personal involvement and significant life changes.

A. A simple imaginative placing of yourself in the biblical scene, in which the leader guides you through a series of questions and exercises, that results in a variety of personal decisions.

B. A much more carefully organized approach, described by Walter Wink in *Transforming Bible Study,* which ventures into the psyche of the participant through well-designed questions and the use of physical and emotional tools.

APPROACH A
Making Biblical Stories Your Story

One of the most incredible discoveries is when "the Story" in the Bible becomes your story! It happens when the story about Adam and Eve's temptation, sin, and guilt turns around and grabs you, and you suddenly realize that the truths of that ancient narrative are really truths about you. When Jesus' parable about the good Samaritan ceases to be just an interesting piece of literature nearly 2,000 years old, and you or I realize that every day we are faced with the dilemma of what to do about the wounded person, and how prone we are to justify our neglect for one reason or another.

One of the Bible study approaches that seeks to achieve this result has been made very appealing to me by W. J. A. (Bill) Power, Episcopal priest and longtime professor of Old Testament at Perkins School of Theology. Dr. Power tells me that he learned the use of this approach in class from Charles R. Fielding, late Dean of Divinity, Trinity College, University of Toronto, Canada. I have earlier told of Dr. Power in the chapter on Theological Bible study, and he usually combines that approach and this one in his insightful and sensitive Bible classes. Although many others also lead such Bible study, I will follow the basic suggestions of Bill Power, a friend and colleague.

Choose character stories in which there are a number of different roles interacting with one another. Many of the narratives of Genesis are excellent, as are stories about Jesus and various groups of people, or many of Jesus' parables.

The key to this approach is imagination. Imaginatively projecting yourself back into the dynamics of the narrative and finding yourself feeling, as well as thinking in the incident described. There is little "about" in this approach because the emphasis is on "involvement with" the text, and with others.

A skillful speaker can do much of this process through rhetorical questions, and suggested mental imagining in a lecture, but it is far better to use the following group processes, if at all possible.

PROCEDURE

Study of Luke 5:1-11: The calling of Simon Peter, James, and John.

1. Divide the class into groups of three.
2. Be sure everyone has a Bible. Ask them to read the passage to themselves in silence.
3. Ask everyone to read the eleven verses again in silence, this time looking for sounds, smells, sights, touches, and even tastes. After all persons have thought (and possibly written) by themselves, ask them to share in their groups of three. You will then want to have some sharing from the small groups, developing a cumulative list, which will probably include sound of the water, smell of the water, smell of the fish, sound of the crowd, smell and press of the crowd, sounds of the boats, sounds of birds around the boats, sweat of the working fishermen, voices (possibly swearing) of the fishermen, Jesus' voice speaking to the crowd, Peter's excited and frightened voice, and so on.
4. As you develop the joint list from the participants, your reading and insights as the teacher may be "worked into" the whole, as you affirm their contributions, and make those of your own. (You will, of course, have done these exercises yourself in your preparation, as well as made use of several biblical resources, which will add to the whole.)
5. Ask the participants to read the passage for the third time, choosing to pretend they are in one of four categories:

    (a) One of the crowd
    (b) Simon Peter
    (c) James or John
    (d) One of the other fishermen

Note: In such exercises there is often a strong tendency for several to want to identify with Jesus, rather than one of the other categories. You should not allow anyone to do this because it is a means of escaping the imperatives of seeing, hearing, and meeting Jesus as did those in his audience.

Ask all persons to imagine how they felt, what were their fears, what they might have seen, how they felt toward Jesus, what they hoped would happen, how they felt toward the others who were present. They may want to jot some of their feelings down on a piece of paper as they reflect.

6. In the original groups of three, ask the participants to share with one another which of the four roles they chose and why. How did they relate to the characters whose role they did not choose?

7. Ask each category to get in a new group together—the crowd, Simon Peter, James or John, the fishermen.

In those groups ask persons to share why they chose the role they did, and why they did not choose one of the other characters. Ask, How do you feel? Do you wish you had done something differently? In what ways do you feel vulnerable? In doubt? glad? surprised?

When using this approach, Bill Power says he is very careful to keep any participant from "over-exposing him or herself" and running the risk of considerable embarrassment. He therefore moves on to someone else when individuals seem to be getting too introspective about their choices and feelings. (This is in sharp contrast to Approach B, which follows.)

8. After some general sharing in the whole class, the

leader should lead a discussion on discipleship and risk. The new disciples were undoubtably taking considerable risks. What might have been in their minds? How do others react when they see someone about to take such a significant step? How would you react? What would a discipleship risk look like for you? What were the risks of those who did not choose to follow Jesus?

9. Ask all participants to write individually a discipleship risk in which they are ready to commit themselves. Suggest it may well be a rather short-term choice that may be done in the next day or so.

Some teachers may want to suggest a brief role play of part of the verses, asking the participants to imagine the conversation, perhaps, when Simon Peter says he is going to go with Jesus. What might he say to the other fishermen? What might they say to him?

Many youth and adults will shy away from this much sharing of feelings. They may want to return to the other realm of ideas and understanding. The teacher will need to smile a lot, and gently nudge the class along.

This approach can be fun, interesting, informative, and even life-changing, at least to a modest degree. One of the great benefits of this approach is that no one is really "wrong," because all are working with their own hunches and feelings, and those are valid in and of themselves.

This approach can, and often should be, included with or as a part of several of the other approaches described earlier. It leads well into Theological Bible study and can easily be used in Depth Bible study (step 2) and Shared Praxis Bible study (step 3).

APPROACH B

A variation on this type of "whole person involvement" is that described by Walter Wink in his book *Transforming*

Bible Study (see Bibliography). Over many years since serving in the pastorate at Hitchcock, Texas (where we were friends), teaching in a theological seminary, and experiencing life-changing insights and feelings at the Guild for Psychological Studies in San Francisco, California, Wink has developed his own version of Bible study. While utilizing the insights of modern biblical scholarship, Wink's emphasis is not on learning about the text, but like that of Power, is primarily concerned with participants becoming involved with their senses, their feelings, their imaginations, and their wills.

Like Power, Wink concentrates on the types of narratives in the Old and New Testaments that have a situation with a variety of characters. Wink has adapted and modified a carefully chosen sequence of questions from the Guild for Psychological Studies, which attempt to lead the participants deeper and deeper into personal involvement and insight, using the text. In many respects this is a much more highly developed procedure than A that parallels Depth Bible study, in chapter 3, and is similar to Dialogue and Encounter in chapter 6.

Dr. Wink has irritated many biblical scholars by saying that current biblical scholarship is out of touch with the local church and contributes little to the life of the individual Christian. Some would even question whether what Wink does is really Bible study at all. They would say he only uses the Bible as a resource for psychological insight, personal change, and growth.

This approach demands the leadership of a very well-prepared teacher who has studied a biblical passage with great care, and I would suggest the teacher also needs to have considerable training in psychological insight. In his book, Wink gives several samples of suggested questions for particular biblical passages, each list carefully planned for a sequence that leads from the passage itself to the life of each participant. Nevertheless, he urges teachers to develop their own questions, and the experience of those who have used this approach confirms the value of this suggestion:

Wink describes this procedure as having three processes or movements:

1. A careful look at the critical issues in the text, seeking to uncover the original meaning of the scripture passage.

2. Amplification, in which questions are developed that bring the participants "into the text," helping them experience the thoughts and emotions of the persons in the story.

3. Application exercises, in which each person is helped to apply the passage to his or her own life, and to make responses that include some kind of follow-through and decision.

(Wink holds regular workshops to train leaders, usually pastors, to lead this kind of Bible study.)

Typical questions used by this approach are found in his treatment of the Healing of the Paralytic, found in Mark 2:1-12, and parallel passages. The questions start quite objectively with, For what purpose did the friends bring the man to Jesus? and, What did they do when they could not reach Jesus?

Several questions later, Wink shifts the emphasis to an attempt to lead the participants to try to fathom Jesus' mind by asking, Why does Jesus speak of forgiveness? The questions then move to the very personal: Who is the paralytic in you? and, What aspects of yourself need the healing offered in this story?

One of the things that makes Wink's approach somewhat unique is that it always concludes in some action that attempts to include the whole person—mind, feelings, and body—in the process. Thus in the passage on the paralytic, the class members are asked to fashion their paralytic in clay, which is provided. Such an experience can be quite emotional, and calls on a very supportive class, and an insightful teacher. The purpose, of course, in such an exercise is to study a biblical passage in such a way that deep aspects of the personal life are not only addressed, but are also released and changed in the process. This is clearly a bold attempt to extend Jesus' healing power through the Holy Spirit in our midst.

Wink urges teachers to resist the temptation to insert (lecturettes) of information at any point in the entire process, and to depend instead almost entirely on the questions they have prepared. However, several persons who have taken the training and used the approach, say that their leadership style is helped when they lecture briefly.

Experienced Bible teachers will realize, of course, that they have used similar questions without such clear goals and planning, and that such questions are indeed a vital part of the application of the gospel. At the same time, it is not easy to handle creatively the emotion-laden responses that are often brought forth. Nevertheless, such approaches to Bible study, which move beyond the mind itself and incorporate the whole person, are often rich experiences. Although few of those using Wink's approach have testified to what they would call "transforming" experiences, many have said that significant changes and growth were indeed quite apparent.

Attempts to role-play, act out, or dramatize such portions of Scripture have long been recognized as important ways to involve children, youth, and adults in incorporating the gospel message into their lives (see chapter 14).

My experience indicates that youth of all ages are quite capable of using Power's approach, but only older youth could do as well with the approach of Wink.

8

You Use Spectrum Bible Study

- ■ —How great a difference there is in the ways Christians understand the Bible!
- ■ —Many of us have changed our understanding during our lifetimes.
- ■ —Understanding those differences and the reasons behind them is very educational.
- ■ —Conflicts and mistrust among Christians can be reduced by studying these differences.

Have you, like me, been brought to tears by the ways "those other people" understand the Bible? How frustrating it is that God in His wisdom allows so many strange people to interpret the Bible in ways I do not approve! But stranger yet, to me at least, is that many of "those" people consider me the most strange and even un-Christian of all, because of the way I interpret parts of the Bible. What is worse, over the years Christians have hated one another and even killed one another because of differences in understanding the Bible.

What are some ways in which we can come to understand one another better in this regard? "Education" has been defined at times as an understanding of:

—the questions
—the answers
—the reasons through history

In regard to any subject, such knowledge gives you a broader perspective, which helps us understand "those strange other people who believe differently than we."

One interesting way to examine such information is for a teacher to develop and present, or work out with a class, a "spectrum" of different points of view. This spectrum will probably move from one extreme to the opposite with several alternatives in between.

To do this, of course, you are facing the reality that Christians have understood the meaning of Scripture very differently, both in the past and in the present. In their own minds they justify their understanding with reasons that are quite meaningful to them. A very important aspect of Bible study therefore is an attempt to understand their reasons, and not simply to be "turned off" by their answers, which may be totally unsatisfactory to you.

To accomplish this goal you must, of course, use a variety of commentaries, including those from both historical-critical scholarship, and those that question much of this scholarship from a more literalistic point of view. Some commentaries list a wide variety of options before choosing the one they find most satisfactory.

In seeking these various understandings, it is important to try to resist the temptation to place either people or positions in neat little boxes with labels they may find distasteful.

As an example of the Spectrum approach, it is possible to develop a spectrum of views of the book of Jonah.

Ways the book of Jonah has been understood.

(Several of these points of view are discussed in the *Interpreters' One-Volume Commentary on the Bible,* pp. 480ff.)

1. For some, the book of Jonah describes an actual historical event that happened exactly as it is described. For

these persons, this must be believed exactly as it is because everything in the Bible must be believed if its authority as the Word of God for Christians is to be solid and dependable. This is simply one of God's miracles.

2. Other Christians believe quite the opposite—the book of Jonah is a good story and only a good story. The story undoubtably came out of ancient lore and was the basis of many a laugh as it was told over and over around the campfire. The story is not actually to be believed by any intelligent person. To try to make anything more out of it than a story is simply foolish.

3. For many of the early church fathers, the book of Jonah was a good allegory. Each part of the story stood for something else in biblical times. Thus,

Jonah is Israel.
The large fish is Babylon.
Babylon swallows Israel.
The fish spews out Jonah, who is really Babylon sending Israel home from captivity.
Jonah's anger is Israel's impatience at the Gentiles' conversion.

Such allegorical interpretations have been used with many parts of the Old and New Testaments over the centuries by many of the church fathers.

The rationale is that since they firmly believe this is God's Word, it has to mean something significant. Since to them it is obviously meaningless as it stands, it must be allegorized to serve its proper function as part of God's message. Furthermore, for Christians in the second and third centuries, such an allegorization would appear to be "obvious." Here again, it is assumed the story is not an actual historical event.

4. For other Christians this is a wonderfully powerful parable telling one of the great spiritual truths of life—that God's persistence, compassion, and mercy are unlimited and often mysterious. The book of Jonah is a wonderful leap of insight by a postexilic Old Testament writer who is breaking out of the bonds of Hebrew nationalism. A story form or parable is used to carry these insights, but it is not to be taken as a historical event, and in fact is told with a good deal of humor.

For many Christians, this parable hits them directly, and they feel "God breathing down their neck" as they try to avoid doing God's will in their lives.

Of course, other Christians have additional understandings of this interesting book of the Old Testament.

ONE PROCEDURE FOR SPECTRUM BIBLE STUDY

1. Assign in advance, or take time in class, for all participants to read the book, chapter, or selected verses for themselves.

2. Ask the class to think about the different ways they have heard Christians interpret the meaning of the section under consideration and list these on the chalkboard. You may want to use a line to represent the spectrum of points of view, such as this for the book of Jonah:

Story Only	Spiritually True	Allegorical	Literal

3. Then more in either a lecture or through guided research by the class members, clarify, add to, modify, and organize the data you have found.

4. Lead the class to explore seriously each point of view

(no matter how strange it seems to the members), asking such questions as—

What is this point of view actually saying?
What values is this position attempting to uphold?
What are some problems with this view?
What are some of the implications of this viewpoint?

If there are persons in the class who strongly identify with one of the points of view, ask if they wish to explain or defend their understanding.

If there is no one in the class who holds one of the positions, you or someone in the class may wish to try to represent that viewpoint as carefully as possible.

5. It will become apparent that the understanding of various members of the class will have changed over the years, sometimes radically. As their faith has gone through development, and as they have faced a variety of life changes, so has their understanding of scripture changed.

Some members of the class may want to reflect on: How my mind has changed in my understanding of this passage, and how that change has resulted from or contributed to my faith development. You, as the teacher, may want to do the same.

If this is done, it is important that the class be asked to be active listeners, seeking to clarify and understand the person's explanation. The class should not try to prove that what is described is invalid or wrong.

Nevertheless, various class members (including the teacher) may wish to say, "Well, right now, today, my understanding is about here on the spectrum, and I like it," while others may take a contrary position.

ADDITIONAL COMMENTS

This is serious, advanced Bible study, requiring an open class that is ready to stretch its understanding and faith.

Toleration of a wide variety of viewpoints is essential, and even a desire to know what is behind other positions is important.

Some persons require a definite answer for such issues, and can become very upset with this approach to Bible study.

This approach can be used with seniors in high school, but is especially suited to young adults, college students, and other more mature adults.

Possible scripture passages suited to this approach include Old Testament narrative stories such as the creation stories, Garden of Eden, Tower of Babel, Noah's Ark, Moses and the Burning Bush, and the Exodus. In the New Testament are the miracle stories, such as Feeding the Five Thousand, Jesus Walking on the Water, Turning the Water into Wine, and so on. Also, there is the book of Revelation.

This approach can be made a part of several other approaches at appropriate points (see especially chapters 3 and 20).

The truth is that Christians have understood the meaning of Scripture (and before this, the events themselves) in many different ways, both in the past and in the present. Both Testaments themselves reveal such differences. This important lesson can be made graphic through Spectrum Bible study.

If this lesson *is* learned, then the church and the churches can begin approaching one another in the spirit of pride and humility. This is genuine ecumenism, one that looks for unity in diversity. Differences must be recognized and accepted, not merely tolerated or condoned. One must have the vision to see in these differences a deep abiding unity. Jesus' words, "That they may all be one . . . ," are both cause and effect throughout the process.

9

You Use Paraphrase and Reverse Paraphrase

- ■ —Putting a passage into your own words often strengthens understanding.
- ■ —Reversing the meaning of selections of Scripture can uncover deep emotions that undergird the passage.
- ■ —Paraphrasing forces one to think carefully about meanings and values of various words.

PARAPHRASING

Readers have been putting the Bible into their own words since the days the scriptures were first written. It is a method essential to learning. As individuals seek words and phrases that express essential meanings, but modify the text sufficiently for the passage to make better sense to them, they are moving toward making the passage their own.

Paraphrasing should be done in writing by all class members, who therefore need pencils and paper. The passage to be paraphrased should include a complete idea, and possibly an entire chapter, such as I Corinthians 13.

Encourage the class to be both faithful to the meaning as they understand it, but also to be rather free with the words they use, not trying to include or follow the exact words as they appear in the Bible before them, but instead concentrating on the ideas.

Paraphrasing is sometimes done by the teacher within the context of a lecture where the teacher reads the passage from one or more translations, and then gives his or her paraphrase as a comparison. This can also be used as a way of modeling what the teacher would like the participants to do later with another selection of Scripture.

Paraphrasing can be used at some point in nearly any of the approaches to Bible study with either youth or adults. There are some useful paraphrases of portions or the entire Bible that have been published. Among them are *The Living Bible*, by Kenneth Taylor, *The Gospels*, and other volumes, by J. B. Phillips, and *The Cotton Patch Version of Paul's Letters*, by Clarence Jordan.

REVERSE PARAPHRASE

This method may have been used widely, but I have never found it in print. In working with three hundred Sunday school teachers in Florida several years ago, I was seeking a new way to get into very familiar passages of Scripture, so I decided to try writing each verse of the 23d Psalm, with the reverse meaning—just the opposite of what the author intended.

As you engage in this quite painful process with such a familiar passage, you begin to realize that the psalmist must have had many such negative feelings and thoughts during his lifetime to have been enabled to write the majestic and wonderful words of the Psalm as we know them. Thus this process leads the participant into similar feelings and thought processes as those actually engaged in by the author.

Warning: When you ask people to do this exercise, you can get quite negative reactions from some persons. They may feel they are doing violence to Scripture, or almost being blasphemous. Some may weep as they work. If some persons say they simply cannot do it, they should always be allowed to just listen.

Some reverse paraphrases are very imaginative and powerful, while others are quite simple.

One of my students wrote the first portion of the 23d Psalm, "God is my jailor. He locks me in a steel cell where I sleep on the floor with rivets every ten inches under my back." A more straightforward reverse paraphrase of Psalm 23 might be:

The Lord is not my shepherd. In fact He always seems to lead me astray.
I am in constant need.
God makes me lie down on very dry ground with a cactus for a pillow.
He leads me into rushing and dangerous water.
God disturbs my soul.
He leads me into the worst kinds of temptations—seemingly just for the fun of it.
When I am afraid of death I know God will be no help.
He leaves me when I need Him and my cane is always four inches too short.
When my enemies show up God leaves me with no protection.
God pours scorn on my head, and my cup is always empty.
Surely trouble and uncertainty will be with me till I die,
And the door to God's presence will always be closed to me.

—(Author's reverse paraphrase)

Another rather startling and certainly thought-provoking reverse paraphrase was written by a pastor in Oklahoma:

73

THE LORD IS MY PARENT

The Lord is my Parent.
I have everything he wants me to have and nothing I need.
He never lets me rest and be quiet and leads me to always overachieve.
He makes me tired!

He guides me in what he thinks is right for me and promises: "Do as I tell you to do and you will be happy."
Only I am never happy.

I am afraid! Even in my sleep he is there to push me where I do not want to go and there is nothing to protect me from falling.

He makes me eat "right" and everyone laughs at me because of what I can not eat or can not drink. I feel like a stranger in my own home.

I am afraid he is ruining my life and I will never escape from him. And this house will be my prison and my life will be too long.

PROCEDURE AND EQUIPMENT

Although paraphrasing or reverse paraphrasing a verse or two can be done through informal discussion, it is usually best to have pencils and paper and, of course, Bibles for each person in the class.

Give each person adequate time to work individually, although you can rarely wait for the last person to finish.

It is best to divide your class into groups of three or four, certainly no more. In sanctuary pews, you should suggest pairs or trios simply working together on the pew.

Ask each person to read his or her paraphrase or reverse paraphrase aloud to the group without comment, until all in the group have been read.

After all have been read, ask the groups to explore the interesting differences between the work of different individuals. Suggest comments, such as: I was especially interested in your third line—why did you write that? or, Your second phrase frightens me, (or startles me, or interests me)—what is behind it?

Ask the groups to avoid comparing similarities and saying, "Yours is about like mine." In this exercise, remember, my "strange" difference from you is my contribution to you. Magnify the interesting differences.

You may have some sharing of individual work with the entire class, but most of the valuable learning is done in the small groups. Each group may want to choose the work of one of its members to be shared with the entire class.

The teacher should read his or her own work as well, but no attempt should be made to agree on the words of just one version.

Note also that sharing feelings and thoughts is a very important form of "debriefing," especially for reverse paraphrasing.

The time schedule for reverse paraphrasing of the 23d Psalm might be—

3 minutes for reading the 23d Psalm from the Bible.

10 minutes for individual writing of the reverse paraphrase.

15-25 minutes during which groups of three or four share and discuss their paraphrases.

10-20 minutes for general sharing in the entire group and concluding remarks of the leader.

While paraphrasing can be done with nearly any portion of the Bible, and in a short time-period if desired, reverse paraphrasing is best with especially familiar portions of Scripture, and at least an hour should be allowed, often an hour and a half.

Good passages for reverse paraphrasing are:

23d Psalm
Lord's Prayer (Matt. 6:9ff.)
Beatitudes (Matt. 5:2ff.)

75

Ten Commandments (Exodus 20)
I Corinthians 13

All of these familiar passages need the "slowing down process" that reverse paraphrasing provides.

STRENGTHS AND LIMITATIONS

The major strength of reverse paraphrase is involvement. The major limitation is possible distortion. Some persons gain great insights and go away excited from this kind of study; others are puzzled and unimpressed. The leader should expect both reactions.

One teacher who used this method of reverse paraphrase of the 23d Psalm with a class of twenty-six young adults reported great interest among participants. In the discussion, most attention was focused on the issue of God's will, and the class did not have time to deal with all the problems raised.

Youth, especially junior high, sometimes find reverse paraphrasing quite difficult, although if they once "get into it" it can be rewarding.

I have used both paraphrasing and reverse paraphrasing with groups of ten to one thousand. The role of the teacher is primarily organizer of the experience, although the teacher may also do considerable modeling (of his or her own) and critical reflecting.

10

You Use Memorization for Adults and Youth

■ —Being able to turn to significant passages of Scripture in one's mind over the years is very important for Christians.

■ —Although memorizing is easier in childhood, it is also possible for youth and adults when they are adequately motivated.

■ —The Bible that is truly yours is the Bible you have in your head rather than the one in your hand.

Memorization has suffered from a bad press. Far too often memorization has been associated with "meaningless memorization" or "trivial memorization." Furthermore, in the past, reciting individually "to prove you know it" has led to either humiliation for some who do it poorly, or false pride for those who do it well. Nevertheless, I believe that memorizing is one valuable aspect of teaching the Bible to adults and youth.

During World War II, I was sitting alone in a foxhole for several hours, with much time on my hands. Rashly, I decided to review the portions of the Bible that I knew by memory—thinking it would take a good long period of time. Unfortunately, it did not. Despite my many years of perfect attendance at Sunday school, and having taught a class for several years before entering the service, I was through with my review long before I wished.

The 23d Psalm and the 95th Psalm came to mind at once, as did the Lord's Prayer and the Beatitudes (I stumbled on some of them), and I was quite good on the Ten Commandments from Exodus 20. Next came the thirteenth chapter of I Corinthians, and part of the fifteenth chapter of the same book, although my memory of both was far from perfect. I had the first several verses of Genesis 1 pretty well in mind, as well as parts of the first chapter of the Gospel of John. I could remember the primary story line of many narratives in the Old and New Testaments, but few correct details. Then, with a few isolated "memory verses," I was through.

That was my Bible! What is *yours?*

Some may ask, Why is it so important to know any of the Bible from memory at all? What good does it do you? Are you a better Christian just because you can recite some scripture from memory? Furthermore, those who are always quoting scripture are just showing off or trying to put the rest of us down!

My answer is clear and direct. I need to know many portions of Scripture from memory to live and to die by. Such knowledge of portions of the Bible gives me a ready reservoir from which to draw both in the day and in the night—both when life is very good, and when life is pretty bad. I also need that knowledge in order to make sense of much that I hear and read.

For me, it is usually much more important to memorize significant portions of Scripture than isolated verses, but there are, of course, exceptions. At times Bible study can be helped by knowing things about the Bible, rather than the words themselves.

About a year ago, while teaching an adult Bible class of about thirty persons in a small church in Colorado, I asked them to memorize six key Old Testament dates. The majority in the class were in their sixties, several in their seventies.

The purpose of memorizing the dates was to give a basic framework for the nearly 800-year period in the Old Testament from the Exodus to the Exile.

Realizing that some of the dates are approximate, we worked on—

1250 B.C.—Exodus, Moses
1009 B.C.—David, United Kingdom
930 B.C.—Division of North and South, Israel and Judah
722 B.C.—Fall of Israel
586 B.C.—Fall of Judah, Exile
538 B.C.—Fall of Babylon, End of Exile

Some knowledge of these dates and this sequence allows a student to hold many of the events and persons of the Old Testament in perspective.

ONE PROCEDURE FOR SUCH MEMORIZATION:

Memorizing depends on creative, varied repetition

1. The teacher goes over the dates and events, talks about them some, and writes them on a chalkboard.
2. Each participant writes the dates and events on a piece of paper, along a time line.
3. The teacher leads the class in unison in a recitation of each date, in chronological order, slowly, and then repeats this, all in good humor.
4. All persons study the list in silence, repeating the dates to themselves.
5. The teacher asks the class to divide into pairs, who then question each other about their lists, with the lists covered. (There is a lot of laughter and fun.)

6. Individuals are invited to *volunteer* to try to recite the entire list. (*No* pressure is put on anyone.)

7. The teacher invites questions, and responds to "flesh out" the events and persons, in order to place them in a broader historical setting.

8. Everybody repeats the list again in unison, which is repeated at the beginning of the lesson the next week.

Such a procedure can be used to memorize any portion of Scripture and as a part of several of the other approaches described in this book. Certainly the scripture passages that I knew (to some degree!) in the army and many others would be valuable to include.

A year from now will the members of the class be able to recite what they have "Learned"? A few will, many will not, but most will be able to pick up the material more readily than if they had never worked on it.

RULES FOR YOUTH AND ADULT MEMORIZATION

1. Use a short body of material.
2. Use material that makes sense and seems worthwhile to the participants.
3. Keep the memorization fun and non-embarrassing.
4. Create many different ways to repeat the material, but be sure to repeat and repeat.
5. Youth like contests, so let them compete, especially as small groups.
6. Older adults can learn nearly anything, but it does take more time.

11

You Use Biblical Scholars

- ■ —Biblical scholars are now available to local churches as never before.
- ■ —Audio and video cassettes, and closed circuit and cable TV can bring any biblical expert into the classroom.
- ■ —Always available in written form, such scholars now appear as "personalities," with great emotional impact.
- ■ —The use of these biblical scholars can have both positive and negative impacts, and scholars must be "kept in their place."

"Friends, this morning we have as our guest speaker one of the most renowned and respected biblical scholars in the world. Please sit back and listen carefully to Dr. William Barkley, who though dead for many years, is with us in our class, thanks to this cassette, made several years ago, in which Dr. Barkley interprets for us some of the parables of Jesus."

In the 1980s, this statement could be heard in even the smallest, most remote church, thanks to inexpensive (often less than $8) audio cassettes now readily available for hundreds of biblical scholars throughout the world. In addition, for a few dollars more, the same scholar may be both seen *and* heard on video cassette. Most churches have members who can lend either their audio or video cassette players for the occasion.

In Shreveport, Louisiana, and several other cities, every Sunday such biblical scholars are brought into many classrooms, by way of closed circuit TV, and at the same time, sent hundreds of miles by way of "down linking" cable to many other churches and classes. How the Sunday morning Bible lesson has changed!

But, wait just a minute, who is studying and teaching the Bible, the scholars or us? In several cities I have visited, which are sites of theological seminaries, pastors in nearby churches complain that the ready availability of seminary professors as teachers for a few classes makes it harder to recruit non-professional teachers for the other classes. Who wants to be compared to a biblical scholar?

The same thing applies, of course, to any use of expert information available in a Sunday school quarterly, a book, or on video cassette. Although the potential for information and inspiration is exciting, we must always guard against this important input limiting the direct consideration of the scripture by the participants themselves.

You will also realize that seminary-trained pastors of most churches are in a real sense the most readily available biblical scholars, whether they consider themselves to be that or not. Therefore, what we say about other scholars also applies to most pastors.

STRENGTHS OF USING A BIBLICAL SCHOLAR

1. A rich store of information gained from years of study.

2. A personal commitment to a lifelong pursuit of understanding the background and complexities of the Scripture.

3. A trained and disciplined imagination, which can often discern connections and implications not available to the average person.

4. An animated and often contagious excitement for the subject, which can be very stimulating to those who hear.

LIMITATIONS OF USING A BIBLICAL SCHOLAR

1. First and foremost, it is easy for most of us to allow scholars to do all the work with the scripture, while we sit back and think, Wow! That is very interesting!

2. Once the scholar has spoken, it is very difficult for many to advance a contrary opinion of their own, even when there is real room for disagreement.

3. The scholar is always speaking from a particular perspective, and often does not acknowledge any possibility of a contrary opinion.

PRINCIPLES TO OBSERVE WHEN USING A BIBLICAL SCHOLAR

1. The scholar will provide information primarily "About" the scripture.

2. If class members are going to get directly "Involved With" the scripture, it will probably have to be before they hear the scholar. *This is very important and is most often ignored.*

Involvement, in which personal opinions, feelings, and points of view are openly shared, is greatly dampened by the authority of a scholar who may be heard first.

Many Bible classes fail to get real involvement because the members have been impressed with the knowledge of the scholar, and do not want to run the risk of being "wrong" because their views are so "uninformed."

It should be remembered that in most churches, on most occasions, the pastor or teacher is the expert.

While some persons take a special delight in arguing with the pastor or teacher (it is sort of fun!), most members of congregations hesitate to *openly* disagree with what a pastor or teacher has just said about a biblical passage, especially if it has been stated with great conviction.

3. The material from the scholar (printed or verbal) should usually be divided into rather short segments, with discussion, clarification, application, and so on, in between. One page of printed material or five to ten minutes of a cassette are usually plenty to discuss at any one time.

For youth this is extremely important, and the segments should usually be shorter rather than longer. For junior high, each section should be very short.

Some speakers or writers "build in" such "digestion" time in what they record or write, so the class can "make the ideas their own," as they go along.

4. Finally, there *are* great advantages to having a scholar available in some form—especially on audio or video—but the scholar's largest contribution is usually "about" the scripture. Teachers should work hard to try to insure "involvement with" the Bible for each person as well.

ONE POSSIBLE PROCEDURE FOR USING A SCHOLAR ON AUDIO OR VIDEO CASSETTE

1. Begin the class by dividing into work groups of three or four persons, assign the biblical text to be studied, and ask the participants to read the passage to themselves, and then discuss it in their groups.

2. Assign specific questions such as:

    (a) What seems to be the major idea or ideas?
    (b) What are some of the key words?
    (c) What additional information do you wish you had?

3. After the groups have worked for ten to fifteen minutes (five minutes for youth), ask for some brief sharing from those who wish to bring out their main ideas or questions.

(Do *not* ask for reports from each group on all that they discussed!)

4. Now, turn on the cassette on which the scholar speaks about the scripture that has just been studied by the group. Play the cassette for five to fifteen minutes or until the natural completion of one section or idea.

5. After hearing from the scholar, ask your class to discuss:

(a) What new insights did you gain from the speaker?
(b) What modifications does this information seem to require of your previous thought and discussion?
(c) What additional information do you wish were available?

6. Such a procedure might be repeated two or three times during an hour's class, with great benefit. (I have often done this with a variety of *Thesis* audiotapes—Box 1124, Pittsburgh, PA 15228—especially with the cassettes of Kenneth Bailey entitled "New Perspectives on the Parables.")

A wide selection of audio and video cassettes is now available at most denominational bookstores, or from their catalogs.

One such high-quality resource is a series of six video cassettes entitled, "The Bible As the Church's Book," and featuring James A. Sandees, Old Testament scholar. Each cassette is in color and is 28 minutes long, but is designed to be used in a 60- to 90-minute informal discussion group. (See Resources at the conclusion of chapter 13 for availability.)

With this procedure, or one somewhat like it, the teacher can lead the class in "involvement with" the biblical text and at the same time utilize the great contribution of a biblical scholar who tells us much "about" the Bible we need to know.

12

You Involve Youth in the Bible

- ■ —Under the "right" circumstances youth are "turned on" to Bible study.
- ■ —Persons who express definite beliefs, are approachable, and are sincerely religious, are those to whom youth respond.
- ■ —"Appropriate" involvement that is both interesting and challenging is welcomed.
- ■ —Leaders must both show respect for the points of view of youth and have a firm faith of their own.
- ■ —Few pastors with whom I have spoken have ever taught a Bible class for youth. I wonder why?

Once upon a time, in a large Houston church where I was one of the pastors, I spent part of many Sunday mornings running four or five high school boys out from behind the furnace in the basement. They liked to go there for a smoke rather than going to Sunday school. We were friends, and I regularly admonished them for not going to their classes. They complained classes were "too boring," and one Sunday one of the boys cracked, "If *you* would teach us the Bible, like you do the adults, we would come and really learn!" I replied, "Oh yes, well, get a group and come to my house next Wednesday night and be prepared to stay two hours!" It was the middle of July.

I did not know if anyone would come, and was surprised

when four of the boys showed up with four girls. I had a supply of Bibles, we sat around the living room, and I said, "We will start in the book of Genesis. Turn to Genesis 1:27-28."

They did so, and we read, "So God created man in his own image, in the image of God he created him; male and female he created them. And God blessed them, and God said to them, 'Be fruitful and multiply, and fill the earth and subdue it; and have dominion over the fish of the sea and over the birds of the air and over every living thing that moves upon the earth.' "

And then I said, "Well, what are you doing about it?" The room instantly burst into an unrestrained babble—everyone was talking at once! I could hardly keep order.

For the rest of that evening and the next three Wednesday evenings, we rather carefully worked our way through much of the first two chapters of Genesis. We discussed at length what it means for a teenager to be made in the image of God, what it means to "have dominion" over the earth, animals, and so on, and the tension between being physically able to have children as teenagers and a society that expects teenagers not to be sexually active until they are married. We discussed Christian discipline, especially as this applies to teenagers, and we talked about the particular temptations of today's society. We also explored the rather incredible concepts that God is both creator and sustainer of all of life, and continues to redeem it as well.

I would read a text, provoke the youth to respond and think (usually in that order!), explain the text itself and ways it was understood, and finally spend a lot of time discussing the implications for them as high school youth, including some possible decisions. Thought and feeling often ran high.

(As you may have recognized, I was using what Tom Groome has come to call "Shared Praxis," [see ch. 5], even though at that time I had never heard the term.)

Pastors—you do not know what you are missing!

The youth of your church are waiting for you, *the pastor,* to imaginatively teach the Bible to them. The payoff—for them and for you—will be far more than you can imagine.

In preparing for this chapter, I interviewed several youth directors, pastors, and lay teachers of youth who have been successful Bible teachers with youth. Their responses were very helpful and form much of what is included.

I must confess that I was surprised and quite dismayed that so few pastors have ever taught the Bible to youth themselves. Calling on those whom I considered the very best, I rarely found a pastor (or Christian educator) who said, Sure, let me tell you how I teach the Bible to youth. Usually they said they included some Bible in confirmation training, and that an occasional youth was in an adult Bible class. But they often said, "Come to think about it, I guess I never have."

How many of these pastors have been suspicious and on edge when youth from their churches took enthusiastic part in Youth for Christ, or Campus Crusade Bible study groups? Maybe those groups were the first opportunity these young people ever had to study the Bible with a trained Bible leader. The mainline churches must reclaim the Bible for their youth, and pastors are usually the key to doing so.

SOME MYTHS AND REALITIES

Myth—Youth have learned the basic stories of the Bible as children and are now ready to explore their deeper meanings.
Reality—Most youth, in most churches, know little about the Bible. It is a mistake to assume that because they have attended Sunday school for several years, they will be able

to recall or utilize much biblical information. (This was a 100 percent agreement of persons working with youth.)

Myth—Youth are not really interested in Bible study.
Reality—Most youth who come to churches (and many who do not) *will* respond to Bible study *eagerly* if they are involved with the Bible by a *vitally* interested adult.

Myth—Youth always want a young person or young adult to teach and lead them. Anyone over thirty need not apply!
Reality—The best youth leaders are not necessarily the young adult, but instead any age adult who is open and interested in youth, and has a vital, growing faith. Such adults are able to share their faith, and at the same time allow youth to develop their own faith; they do not feel compelled to stuff their adult faith down the throats of the youth.

Myth—Youth respond best to church programs that stress "fun and games" not those that "get involved in Bible study and serious stuff."
Reality—Youth are very interested in religion today, and want their interest to be taken seriously by the church and adults. They do, of course, enjoy fun things and ski trips, but these pursuits are not at the heart of their interests.

SOME GENERAL PRINCIPLES

1. Youth expect adult leaders to be interested in them as persons, and where possible, "to be in touch with their world." At the same time, youth do not want adults to pretend that they are still youth, but to be mature persons with youthful spirit. It is not necessary to be able to squat down on the floor to be a good leader of youth. In fact, a confession of what an adult can no longer do physically is a

good reminder to youth of the nature of aging, and is no deterrent to being well-liked and respected by youth.

2. Several youth leaders have said it is a mistake for adults to expect a lot of verbal praise and "strokes" from youth. Expressions of thanks will be rare, and may come in a look or a gesture, rather than words.

3. Youth leaders with whom I spoke agreed that most young people anticipate that adults will often not tell them the truth. Basic candor is very important in working with youth.

Leaders should try to tell how they really feel, what their points of view are, their attitudes toward things going on in the world, of what they are *really* going to allow the youth to do, and so on. This is especially true of the Bible and of Christian faith and practice. Of course, this does not mean that adults "dump" all their feelings and doubts inappropriately on the young people in their class or group.

4. Youth usually need time to "debrief" their daily interests and concerns by free-wheeling talk of school, sports, dates, and so forth, before the leader tries to get serious. Adult leaders should also not be surprised if the transition from one to the other is not complete when it is requested.

5. Bible study sessions should be relaxed and fun. Being able to laugh at oneself, and to see the humorous aspects of daily life and biblical stories is a great asset. At the same time, youth need and expect *order*, and some discipline, and depend on adults to provide at least part of it.

6. When youth get quite out of line, and break rules you consider important, do not assume that they are attacking you, insulting you, or rejecting your leadership. Young people are often, if not usually, reacting to forces in their lives that are outside the immediate environment of the class or the church.

7. Only exceptional teachers can give interesting lectures to youth that last more than a few minutes. Information

needs to be presented in a wide variety of ways, most of which involve youth actively. Short, modular segments of material and structure are often the best way to move through a lesson. I will often view a 45-minute lesson as three modules of 15 minutes each.

8. As young people mature from junior high to senior high, they are ready to assume more and more leadership of their own groups, including study of the Bible. We are mistaken to assume this will be true of fellowship or service groups, but not of class on Sunday morning.

I believe J. David Stone's "Four Phases of Ease" (from *The Complete Youth Ministries Handbook*, vol. 1, Nashville: Abingdon, 1979) is essential for success in youth leadership. Adults dare not leave out any of his steps:

1. I do it—you watch.
2. I do it and you do it.
3. You do it, and I'll support and supervise.
4. You do it.

This would apply to any of the approaches to Bible study described in previous chapters.

WAYS TO INVOLVE YOUTH IN BIBLE STUDY

We must always remember that "involvement" does not mean talking. Many persons talk to keep from really getting involved, either mentally or emotionally. Many quiet youth become very involved with both their minds and their feelings without saying a word. The teacher must judge the quantity and quality of involvement on other bases than the sound of voices.

1. In-Class Silent Reading

Today's youth are very uneven readers. Some are excellent, some are poor. In Bible study we are not testing reading ability, and every teacher in the church should avoid embarrassing a young person for his or her inability to read well.

This means that reading the scripture or lesson aloud around a circle, each person being called on in turn, is an absolute "No, No"! Far better either to read in unison, or ask the class to read a paragraph or two in silence to themselves. This means, of course, that some will finish much sooner than others, and that some will not finish at all. Nevertheless, all will have read some on their own, and you can begin to ask questions or have a discussion, knowing that each person is somewhat familiar with the material.

2. Subdividing Your Class for Discussion or Work

I was teaching eight tenth graders sitting around a table, and asked a question to which no one replied. I said, "Nudge your neighbor and discuss the question with him or her," and within a few seconds, everyone was talking. That did not mean they were all involved with the subject, but it soon became apparent that several of them were involved and interested.

Creative grouping is one of the most important skills a Bible teacher can possess. Dividing into smaller groups can also get you into trouble. Three rowdy boys in the same small group can invite noise and confusion. That means we should often put youth in groups while carefully choosing who will work with whom. Groups of two or three are, in my opinion, usually far better than groups of four or five, for youth.

3. R and D—Research and Discovery

Research and discovery need not be restricted to big business or industry. Let us use it with youth in teaching the Bible. To do research requires resources: books, tapes, pictures, and so on, or at times research is done with people. Sometimes you may want to introduce an element of competition into the discovery—always, of course, trying to avoid embarrassing anyone.

Example:

Working in pairs, discover four different ways a verse of Scripture has been translated, and two ways it has been paraphrased. What are the differences? What do these differences imply?

Or,

Working in groups of three, find out all you can about the Pharisees in the next fifteen minutes.

To be able to carry out this research, the young people will need to have available a number of Bible translations and paraphrases, as well as a Bible dictionary and concordance (see chapter 23). Such work can be both fun and informative.

How much better, in many instances, than for you to have done the research in advance, and simply told the class what you found.

4. Hooking

I am sure that you know a hook slides in easily, and comes out with difficulty. In teaching the Bible, it is often helpful to look for a "hook" in the material to help catch the attention of the youth. In the opening story of my teaching the Bible in this chapter, my first question to the young people after reading the scripture was, "Well, what are you doing about it?" That question served as a great hook because it immediately brought up the ambiguity of their own sexual drives, and the restraints of our faith and society. It took us immediately into reality.

A hook is often a commonplace given a twist. When are you stronger than God? is asked as a hook. The answer, of course, is when you hold the door of your own heart's response to God. Hooks involve. Develop the skill of looking for and developing hooks, to catch and hold interest.

Two additional ways to involve youth in Bible study are discussed in chapters 13 and 14.

13

You Use Video Cassettes and Biblical Films

- ■ —Rejoice—Give Thanks to God! The days of trying to thread a projector or replace a burned-out bulb in the middle of a film are almost over.
- ■ —The video cassette is rapidly becoming the primary means of projected visual presentation, although films are still needed for large groups.
- ■ —A projected, moving, and speaking visual image of biblical events and persons, well-produced and filmed, can make vivid and alive what had before seemed strange and far away.
- ■ —Nevertheless, such resources usually portray a literal picturization tending to shut off imaginative understanding of story, parable, and poetry.
- ■ —Finding creative ways to use video cassettes and films to teach the Bible is a challenge even to the best teachers.

It was just getting dark as I set up a movie projector in the center of a mobile home park near Paducah, Kentucky. It was 1953, I was a missionary to these families who were building a nearby plant, and I was about to show a filmed episode on the life of Christ. Families came out of their trailers, set up folding chairs and spread blankets, and watched for thirty minutes.

What, if anything, was I accomplishing by showing these films? Were they only entertainment, and not all that good, besides? Was I in any sense "teaching the Bible"? Did they motivate watchers to want to know more? Did they promote serious Bible study? Did anybody learn anything right there? Some watchers said the films "made the Bible come alive" for them. Others said they helped them visualize incidents in Jesus' ministry better than ever before. Several did enroll in the Bible classes we taught every week in the same mobile home park, and the films certainly helped the viewers feel a part of an overall ministry, including weekly worship.

For more than seventy-five years, Bible teaching has been enhanced or hindered by the use of a changing stream of audiovisual equipment. Do you remember the wonderful stereoptician, which used large, glass slides, and could project a page out of a book or magazine? Many of these projectors can still be found in church closets, gathering dust and rarely used, even though they are quite useful.

We have had 16mm projectors, slide and filmstrip projectors, 78, 45, and 33 rpm records, the 8mm projector, audiotapes (first reels and then cassettes), and then video reels and cassettes. What a procession! Many of us are exhausted when we remember what fads we have been through over the years. We should not, of course, forget the useful overhead projector that more than one pastor actually built into the pulpit for use every Sunday. Today we have video cassettes used in closed circuit TV and satellite, or "Christian" network TV, to make vivid the holy Scriptures. What will it be tomorrow? It is anyone's guess.

The advantages of video cassettes are great. When you buy or rent a biblical video cassette, you can simply slip it into a video recorder hooked up to a regular TV set. The need for skill in operating or threading a projector is absent, as is worry about a burned out projection bulb. We have entered a new era in visual projection.

TWO MAJOR PROBLEMS: HOLLYWOOD AND LITERALIZING

A continuing and possibly ever-present problem in using projected materials is that our audience watches several hours of such material, largely for entertainment, on their own television sets each week. Hollywood has produced several commercial films (some now available on video cassette), with the help of millions of dollars, which are intended to dramatize, be exciting, and entertain.

How does the church compete with Hollywood? How do we overcome the tendency of our participants to think, as the projector or television set is turned on, Well, we are going to be entertained today?

I do believe there is only one, partially successful, course of action. We must create our own context for Bible study when we use projected materials. For me, that means using Bibles in class first—turning to the texts, reading, and thinking about them as a class—before we see the video presentation of the biblical event.

Although I do believe we can show biblical films or video cassettes simply for biblical enrichment, I think if they are used in a class for Bible study, we must do more than just show the material and then go home.

Our second major problem is the tendency of most biblical films and cassettes to treat the entire Bible literally. I have always been grateful that the New Testament never tells us what Jesus actually looked like. We do not know his build, his height, the color of his eyes or hair—nothing, thank God! Jesus' looks can fortunately be ignored as people who are black, yellow, brown, and white come to love and worship him.

Most biblical films not only portray Jesus in a particular way, but they also tend to show all miracles, parables, and narratives (even poetry) in the literal words of the text. The many obvious instances, and possible instances, where we may have dreams or dramatic speech (e.g., God descending on Jesus like a dove), or where we simply lack factual data—all call for the use of imagination.

Therefore, whenever we use biblical films or cassettes, the teacher needs to remind the class that even though we have seen it, the event may not have happened exactly that way. In fact, it *has to be* visually distorted. There is no escape. Interestingly enough, the better the production, the more powerful the distortion may be. When the audience sees lightning etch the Ten Commandments on the stone tablets in the MGM production, *The Ten Commandments*, made a few years ago, it is not easy for many people to imagine it happening in any other way. The teacher must work to stimulate the minds of the participants to continue to think of options.

There is a wide variety of biblical films (many now available on video cassettes) listed in various catalogs, and some are quite old (see the end of this chapter). I am going to consider the use of only one of these productions.

THE NEW MEDIA BIBLE

The best example of high-quality video presentations of biblical material, including scholarly support from audiotapes, filmstrips, and booklets, is the *New Media Bible*, produced by a group called the Genesis Project, Inc., begun in 1975.

Originally a series of thirty-three 18-minute episodes on 16mm film, these are now available also on videotape. The films can also be obtained in Spanish. All are in color, with biblical characters acting out what the text says, speaking the characters' native tongue, and narrators such as Orson Welles reading the RSV text.

The videotapes contain four or five episodes each; for

example, #10 contains "The Creation," "Adam and Eve," "Cain and Abel," and "Noah and the Flood."

There are a total of seventeen Old Testament episodes, including four on Abraham, five on Isaac, Esau, and Jacob, and five on the Joseph sagas. The New Testament, all based on the Gospel according to Luke, includes sixteen episodes. They are all available on four 60-minute videotapes, as follows: "Jesus' Birth and Early Life," "Jesus' Miracles," "Jesus' Parables," and "Easter to the Ascension." Availability and sources for these films or tapes can be found at the end of this chapter.

A Model for Using The New Media Bible

NMB #10, "Adam and Eve"—Genesis 2:4–3:24

1. Preview the film or video cassette at least once, possibly twice. Read, listen to, and view the accompanying audiotapes and filmstrips. Develop a plan of procedure based on your own goals and the time available.

2. Ask the class to read Genesis 2:4 through 3:24 to themselves in silence, nothing anything they had not thought of before.

3. Divide the class into pairs (by asking them to "nudge their neighbor") and share their reactions to this reading of the story of Adam and Eve. Guess how the film will depict the scene of their temptation and sin. Think of more than one possibility.

4. Show the 18-minute film.

5. With the entire class participating, lead them in outlining exactly what was shown: first—then—then—and so on.

6. Ask the class to re-read quickly the scripture passage. Were there any apparent discrepancies in the film? Discuss.

7. Ask questions of the class, such as: What surprised

you? What did you find especially interesting? In what ways were you disappointed? What would you have changed? why? Did you ever feel involved? Was this story in any way about you? when?

8. Summarize your understanding of the discussion, and add your own points of view and witness. Lead the class in a prayer of thanks to God for the gift of creation, and our human companions. (If you use step #9, save this step for last.)

(The procedure above can be done in fifty to sixty minutes.)

9. If the class has additional time available, show one of the filmstrips that came with the film, and work in groups of three to discuss its implications. This will enhance and enlarge the horizons and viewpoints of the class.

YOUTH AND VIDEO CASSETTES

Youth tend to be more critical of video cassettes or films than adults. Youth are accustomed to and expect a great deal of action and professional actors, although Bible videos are often slow-paced, and have actors who are obviously not movie star caliber. There may be hoots and hisses during the films, which should be accepted as youthful reactions to the differences from the video products youth see every day.

Every effort should be made to use the films as educational tools. "Viewing questions" can be assigned in advance—some factual, and the answers should be requested at the end of the film.

The film can be stopped at appropriate places for discussion, before it is completed.

See also other suggestions in the Resources, especially for teaching youth, below. Video cassettes and films can enhance Bible study. Use them in your classes to add to, not detract from, your study.

RESOURCES

For information on the *New Media Bible,* write:
Genesis Project—Media Bible
P.O. Box 37400
Washington, DC 20013

For purchase of videotapes of the *New Media Bible,* write or call:
Gateway Films
2030 Wentz Church Rd.
Box A
Lansdale, PA 19446
   ph. (215) 584-1893

For rental of videotapes of the *New Media Bible,* write or call:
ECUFILM
810 12th Ave. S.
Nashville, TN 37203
   ph. *Toll Free* (800) 251-4091

For the rental of other biblical films and videotapes, write or call ECUFILM above.

For Youth—a very useful resource for teachers of youth is a 36-minute video cassette entitled "Active Learning for Youth—Through Media," which is also available from ECUFILM.

14

You Use Personalized Mental Drama, Role-playing, and Biblical Simulation

■ —The Bible has been described as an "unfolding drama," in which God relentlessly seeks and finds His wayward creatures.

■ —The Bible is full of dramatic incidents and relationships, in which feelings dominate thought.

■ —The dramatic interrelationships in the Bible provide a powerful counterpart to our twentieth-century interrelationships, and actually aid us in improving painful aspects of our daily lives.

■ —There is a progressive degree of emotional involvement from story-telling to case studies, to role-playing, to informal drama, to simulation.

■ —Personalized mental drama can be conducted entirely within a lecture with no one else in the class speaking at all.

■ —Description emphasizes ideas.
Enactment emphasizes feelings.
Description is primarily "About."
Enactment is primarily "Involved With."

■ —It is vital for full Bible study that we teach the Bible in ways that involve the participants in the biblical drama.

IT'S SILLY!

Youth and adults, especially men, often feel silly when asked to "play act" or engage in any kind of dramatic enactment. A typical reaction is, "I came to *learn*, not fool around with feelings!" It is difficult for many persons to realize the extent to which God has always communicated with us through our emotions, as well as through our minds. Nevertheless, the benefits are considerable when adults and youth are helped to relax, smile, laugh, and run the risks of seeming inept.

PERSONALIZED MENTAL DRAMA

A good way to begin is within the minds of each participant. The teacher says, "Imagine yourself in a conversation between the younger and the older brother in Jesus' parable in Luke 15:11-32. First you are the older brother [probably a more natural role for most of us]. What did you say to your brother when he first asked for his share of the estate and then left? How did you feel toward him? Think for a minute—imagine what you thought and felt." Some persons may want to imagine themselves sisters.

At this point, if the teacher wishes, he or she may ask participants to share their thoughts and feelings with *one* other person, but the teacher may ask only for mental responses, responses given solely within the mind of each given person. If so, the teacher must pause long enough for real thought to actually take place. The teacher may also suggest possible responses the class members might be thinking, to stimulate their thought.

The questions of the teacher-lecturer continue: "What do you want to say to your younger brother who has just returned? How do you feel about him and his behavior? How do you feel toward your father? Do you feel like doing something?"

The teacher, pausing after each question, now asks for a reversal of identification: "Now you are the younger brother. Try hard to understand his position and behavior.

What was possibly behind your original course of action? How might you have felt before you left? What did you say to your older brother as you left the house? What do you want to say to your brother, who has been so 'faithful and good,' now that you have returned?"

As you can see, a "mini-drama" can be simulated in each class member's mind without any of the participants saying a word, although many will find it hard to remain silent!

All the teacher needs to do is:

(a) Set the stage.
(b) Ask the questions.
(c) Give time for thought and reflection.

This is what I like to call a "personalized mental drama." I am sure that many of you who read this have done such a procedure to some extent in any number of lessons. This can be very involving and have several participants on the edge of their chairs, begging to share with the class.

ROLE-PLAYING

When the teacher uses personalized mental drama, he or she often finds that several members of the class are now prepared to act out their mental responses in front of the class. The teacher can ask for volunteers to play each of the brothers, again "set the stage" for the "actors," and give them enough time to get beyond their earliest comments. When the first pair are finished, another pair may wish to do their own version. After these role-plays, the entire class should be led in "debriefing" the experience with others in the class, sharing their feelings and thoughts.

Feelings will run high.
Involvement can be great.
The reality of Jesus' parable will be enhanced.

Another possibility is to ask your class to divide into pairs, with each pair role-playing with each other, all at the same time. The teacher says, "Turn to your neighbor, decide who will play which brother, and begin." There will be no need for each pair to "report" on their work, but some will want to talk to the entire class concerning what developed.

(There will be a temptation in some groups to overplay the roles, and become ridiculous—especially in youth groups—but that tendency is usually overcome in a few minutes, and after a few laughs, the class members settle down to more serious enactment of their feelings.)

The teacher needs to follow up such role-playing with further exploration of the depths of the drama. The tension between the "good child" and the "wayward child" is as universal as humankind, and carries over into adulthood for many of us. Have you ever tried settling an estate among several brothers and sisters in their fifties and sixties? The difficulties in coming to a common course of action are unbelievable!

SIMULATION

Biblical simulation is a formal means of enactment, usually with study time to prepare the roles (using the Bible extensively), time for the actual enactment of a biblical event, and finally, adequate time to reflect on what has just happened and its significance. I have found this approach one of the most powerful and helpful of any. I strongly recommend it for your consideration.

A good simulation should take several hours (at least three or four), and is best done on a retreat or during a planned period of extended study. I have often conducted such simulations with two hours of class time for preparation one week, followed by two hours the second week—one for the enactment, and the last hour for reflection on the experience.

Biblical simulations are excellent for high school youth, college students, and young adults. Simulation *can* be used with junior highs, with careful preparation, help from teachers at each point in the process, and a shortened time span. Weekend, Sunday school class retreats, woven around four to six hours for a biblical simulation, can be exciting, and a great deal of biblical learning can take place.

Although imaginative teachers can and do develop their own simulations of the Bible, there are two excellent books that include a variety of carefully developed simulations from both the Old and New Testaments. These are:

Using Biblical Simulations, by Donald E. Miller, Graydon F. Snyder, and Robert W. Neff (Valley Forge, Pa.: Judson Press, 1973); and volume 2, published in 1975. Their subtitle is accurate: "Learning from the Bible by Being There."

The authors define a biblical simulation as "the reenactment of some particular biblical event in an attempt to portray accurately some selected features of that event" (Vol. 1, p. 7).

Each word in the definition is important to our understanding of biblical simulation. It is a *reenactment* (as accurately as possible) of a carefully selected event in which only *some* of its features are attempted to be portrayed, while others are not (such as a carefully designed stage). In my experience, the primary biblical study values are in: (a) getting into the roles as accurately as possible, and (b) experiencing the complexities of the event itself as never before.

The events reenacted may be "closed," a form in which the ending is enacted as it is said to have happened, or the events may be "open," in which the participants can decide for themselves what the outcome will be.

106

For several years I have been using simulation #11 in volume 1 of these books, which is entitled "What Shall We Do With Jesus?" a reenactment of Jesus before the Sanhedrin, taken from John 11:45-53. The authors have generously and thoughtfully provided several tearout pages for each simulation, which the user is encouraged to reproduce freely.

This particular simulation is "open," so that the participants can decide for themselves what they will do with Jesus. There are four "parties" represented equally on the Sandedrin: Sadducees, Pharisees, Herodians, and Apocalypticists. A key aspect of this simulation is careful study to enable the participants to understand their party as thoroughly as possible. While the book gives a thumbnail sketch of the Sadducees, for instance, it also lists several New Testament references where the behavior of the Sadducees is described. Those who are going to be Sadducees are further urged to consult good Bible dictionaries to more closely understand the point of view and concerns of these persons at the time of Jesus.

In my experience, I need to allow at least two hours of class time for serious young adults to prepare for these roles, although I do not take that long for youth.

The reenactments, following the careful directions of the book, are always exciting, and show one how seriously the class members have studied their roles. No one who takes part in such a simulation seriously will ever read John 11 casually again.

Simulation for Another Culture

A few years ago one of my former students from the Fiji Islands used this same simulation for the Bible study of a large gathering of Fiji students from many parts of the world. He mailed the assigned roles in advance to different groups of students, and his instructions were something like this:

"We are going to try a Fiji Jesus before a Fiji Sanhedrin made up of Fiji Pharisees, Fiji Sadducees," and so on.

Here we see a bold attempt to bring an ancient Middle Eastern account of the Jewish trial of a Jewish man to a Melanesian culture (corrupted by Western ways). What a stretch! Finaw, who had gone through this biblical simulation in my course at Perkins, told me the simulation went very well, there was great enthusiasm, and a belief on the part of many that they had gained many new insights into the Bible.

Personalized mental drama, role-playing, and biblical simulation provide unusual opportunities to enrich and make interesting serious Bible study.

15

You Select from and Bring Together Various Approaches in Every Class

■ —None of the approaches just described, or any others, are appropriate to use with every part of the Bible.

■ —Bible study is more interesting and stimulating when a variety of approaches is used.

■ —Often more than one approach may be used in any given class session, helping the participants learn "About"and get "Involved With" the scriptures from different perspectives.

■ —Teaching becomes an art as you develop a "feel" for your own strengths and your classes' responses and interests.

■ —Most of these approaches can be used with denominational Sunday school material by adapting the approaches to fit both the time available and your class. This is always true of the Uniform or International Lesson Series.

OUR PROBLEM

Most classes I visit try to include too much, too fast, too superficially. The teacher's mind often seems to be more on the lesson than on the participants' involvement with the material of the Bible.

At times I want to *escape* to avoid being run over by the "Lesson Express"!

Youthful minds respond more quickly than do adults'

minds, but both groups need to *digest* ideas and feelings, as well as *ingest* them. Unbeknown to many pastors and teachers, many persons leave a class with "mental indigestion." Stuffed with so much information (often good information), many persons throw up their mental hands halfway through, and simply "turn off" what has yet to be digested. How much better to use one story or one verse that the participants can reflect on, feel about, and consider from several points of view.

FACTORS IN SELECTING AND COMBINING APPROACHES

1. *The Scripture you are studying.* Is it a narrative? parable? poetry? laws? argument? prophecy?
2. *Your goals.* What do you want to happen? Learn facts? Discuss various interpretations? Get involved emotionally with a story? Put scripture in your own words? Think theologically? Make personal decisions?
3. *Time.* How much is available? twenty minutes? One-and-a-half hours? Can you arrange to have more?
4. *Size.* How large is the class? What are the possibilities for subdividing the class during part of the lesson?
5. *Room arrangement and equipment.* Are Bibles available? Will people bring their own? Are there surfaces on which participants can write?
6. *The class.* What methods are they accustomed to following in class? What are they willing to try? Will they trust you in doing something different? (Probably more than you think.)
7. *You.* Are you willing to try new approaches? What do you do best? Do you want to try some approaches with other teachers before you do them with your class?

Considering all these factors to some degree, you will ask yourself what approaches you want to use in any one class, or in a series of classes.

You may decide to use Depth Bible study for several weeks, possibly combining it with Approach A in chapter 7, in a class where there is a Bible story good for involving the class with the characters.

For one or more classes you may use theological Bible study, possibly combining it with Approach A in chapter 7, or you may want to include in either of these a paraphrase if it appears it will add to, and not detract from, the lesson.

Others will prefer to use Shared Praxis Bible study consistently, using some other approaches occasionally for variety.

If you are a Sunday school teacher using a regular series of lessons, with suggested procedures each week, the approaches in this book should serve as added options or modifications of what you find in your material.

Methods (or Approaches)
should always serve the
content of the Bible,
never the other way around.

PART II
YOU ARE A PASTOR

You Preach and Teach the Bible

- —Joining the "preached word" and the "taught word" was a practice of Jesus that we observe over and over in the Gospels.
- —Over-ingestion and under-digestion of words, words, words causes "gospel indigestion" in many.
- —Balancing *hearing* the Word with *thinking about* and *feeling into* the Word is an obvious need.
- —Learning and acting out the fruits of the faith are enhanced by considering the same scripture in more than one way.
- —When the pastor both preaches and teaches the scripture, the rewards are enthusiastic responses, observable increases in biblical knowledge, and a surprising growth in the pastor's biblical depth.
- —No pastor has the right not to lead Bible study. Preaching from the Bible is not enough. Preaching biblically is not enough. No matter how many come, or do not come, the pastor *must* regularly organize groups to study the scripture. Jesus said, "Go, teach."
- —Of the many ways available to combine preaching and teaching, the following approaches are more well known. There are, of course, many variations of these, as well as other approaches altogether.
- —Good preaching, in and of itself, often accomplishes several of the goals of classroom Bibly study, but I will leave consideration of that skill to those who do it regularly.

16

You Teach the Bible Through a Congregational Lectionary and Study Groups

- ■ —Most sermons are preached in relative detachment, with neither preparation nor follow-up by the congregation.
- ■ —This approach attempts to strengthen the congregation's understanding of, involvement with, and commitment to the biblical text from which the sermon is preached.
- ■ —Here the biblical text may be studied in three different ways:

    —in a written guide for each family.

    —in a neighborhood study group.

    —in the pastor's sermon the following Sunday.

Used in some form by many congregations and pastors, this approach was made known to many of us in the late 50s and early 60s through the life and writings of the East Harlem Protestant Parish, in New York City.

Described through the books of both George (Bill) Webber and Letty Russel, both pastors in that parish in those years, this approach brings together biblical (lectionary) preaching with some individual study of the lectionary. Individual study is done in quarterly guides and finally in neighborhood lay-led study groups during the week before hearing the sermon, which is based on the scripture studied.

PROCEDURE

1. A congregational lectionary based on one of the commonly accepted lectionaries is followed throughout the year.

2. A small quarterly lectionary guide is written by the pastor, usually devoting two pages to the passages for one week, concentrating on one of the scriptures for that week. This may be a single weekly photocopied sheet or a column in the church paper.

This guide includes some exegesis, some reference to other sources, some direct application to the needs of that parish and its ministry, and suggests provocative questions for discussion, thought, and feelings.

In East Harlem, the guide was written by a clergy member of the parish staff. It included carefully chosen and developed art directly arising from the various texts and the local neighborhood.

These guides were provided every three months to each family in the parish in an inexpensive mimeographed form prepared by members of the parish.

3. The congregation was divided into neighborhood groups of ten to fifteen persons, who met each Wednesday evening for study of the lectionary scripture for that week, using the pages in the guide to stimulate their discussion. The groups met in members' homes or apartments, and a layperson led the discussion.

A key feature of this form of Bible study was that the pastor chose to visit a different neighborhood group each week, and sat and listened to the discussion, not leading, but only participating with the others in the group.

4. On Sunday the pastor preached from the same text studied in the groups the week before. During the sermon the pastor often made reference to some of the particular comments or ideas of the persons who were in the group he or she had visited that week.

I was in the congregation in East Harlem when the pastor

said, "Aunt Sally at Ed's apartment suggested that the implication of this passage for her was _____. Since I heard her say that, I have been over the scripture again, and her comment has caused me to think about _____."

What a powerful way to teach the Bible!

Here the scripture is studied by individuals at home, studied and discussed in a close group, and then proclaimed and taught in the sermon on Sunday—and the lectionary guide is available in the homes of the congregation for future reference.

ADDITIONAL COMMENTS

Some of the neighborhood groups, of course, functioned in splendid ways, although others were either poor or struggled along with little enthusiasm. Even though one may wish that every group could be equally alive and vital, that is rarely the case. In fact, some of the groups simply died out after a few weeks, although others grew stronger and better as time went on.

The writing of the lectionary guide itself required serious study and preparation, and the pastors felt this helped their preaching in and of itself. Some pastors will find this writing a burden, while others will be quite stimulated by it.

Currently, Dr. Zan Holmes and the church he serves, St. Luke's United Methodist Community Church of Dallas, are using their own form of this significant approach to teaching the Bible.

There are fifteen neighborhood groups following the lectionary from which Dr. Holmes preaches every Sunday. He visits a different group each Wednesday, both sharing and listening. Zan is enthusiastic about the vitality of this unified approach to preaching and Bible study, and he says it has had a transforming effect on the congregation.

Here is a fine way for the pastor to magnify the effectiveness of a good sermon.

17

You Teach the Bible While Preparing to Preach

■ —Many pastors acknowledge that preparing the weekly sermon helps keep them from losing their souls! The necessity of exploring a biblical text and allowing it to explore you is a great aid in spiritual vitality. Why should this experience be reserved for preachers?

■ —Seldom are laypersons asked to contribute directly to the pastors' study for the weekly sermon.

■ —This approach to Bible study has a clear purpose, which motivates all involved.

■ —Pastors acknowledge that they are also learners as they sit before the biblical text with members of the congregation.

Some form of this approach has probably been used by pastors for a long time. I first heard of this particular structure of teaching the Bible from William S. Smith, a friend for more than thirty-five years. For many years pastor of Westminster Presbyterian Church, Charlottesville, Virginia, Smith used this approach at Presbyterian churches in Texas during the 1950s and 1960s. I have recommended it often, and many have tried it in one or more congregations.

The pastor organizes a small group, which meets weekly to share in the exegesis of the scripture texts that the pastor will preach on in the weeks ahead.

PROCEDURE

1. The pastor organizes a group of eight to twelve persons to meet weekly to study the scripture text that he or she will preach on in two or three weeks.

2. The text is assigned at the previous meeting so each person can study the scripture in advance and possibly read one or more commentaries.

3. The group meets for an hour to an hour and a half on Saturdays at breakfast, on a week night, or on Sunday evening. The participants are usually seated around a table, with Bibles and books out before them.

4. The discussion begins with a look at the meaning of the words in the text (exegesis), ways in which different commentators have understood those words, and the understanding of the persons in the group.

Discussion then moves to a contemporary understanding of the text, with members of the group sharing their insights. Finally, personal impact and understanding is sought by the pastor. The pastor may ask questions like—

What did you discover about this text? What surprised you? concerned you?

How do you feel about the text? How do you feel about the persons who were involved?

What do *you* believe the author was trying to say?

What does the text mean to you personally?

What would *you* preach about in this text?

The pastor listens carefully, takes notes, and possibly records the responses.

5. Many of these groups include discussions only on the above matters, but others include reflection on the sermon and its use of the text the previous week, and at times the pastor shares her or his outline for the next week, and asks for suggestions or comments.

6. It is quite obvious that the pastor must refrain from turning the sermon over to the group or any members of it. It must be made quite clear at the beginning, and reinforced periodically, that this is joint study of the text, and the preacher will make of it what he or she feels is "right" when it is time for the sermon. Phillips Brooks said that "preaching is truth through personality," and that must not be jeopardized by this kind of study.

It should be noted that the pastors I know who have used this approach have never felt the integrity of their preaching threatened. To the contrary, most of them have felt positively about the experience.

7. Most pastors have used this approach for specific periods of time, and have not done it on and on indefinitely.

Usually the groups have had a rotation plan by which after a period of months some are rotated off, and others brought into the group. This rotation has also usually been resisted, with persons leaving the group quite reluctantly. They have enjoyed and grown from the experience, and are sorry to give it up.

In several instances, the pastor has worked the major administrative group—board, vestry, or session—through the Bible study until all those who are interesed have had an opportunity to participate for a period of weeks or months.

8. Both the "products" and "by-products" of such a plan are quite apparent.

Such Bible study has a specific, visible purpose and result not true of most Bible study. Participants hear and see the results of their work, week by week, in the worship services. This is satisfying.

The pastor and the members of the class come to know each other in a quite different context than through church meetings or worship services. Here they meet one another regularly in the presence of the gospel—in the text of the Scriptures—something many pastors and congregations never experience.

There are also negative possibilities. Some members of the class may feel their points of view are consistently ignored by the preacher, which when there is a radically different theological perspective, may be absolutely true. This is best handled in a straightforward manner of acknowledgment. Others, not involved in the group, may feel excluded, and may resent the pastor paying more attention to some than to them.

Nevertheless, this is an unparalleled form of pastoral education. Involvement with the pastor is one of the significant tasks of the church, and these laypersons have experiences with and insights into the Scriptures as never before.

At one time, I heard that a few of the pastors who led such groups actually preached better sermons, but it was only an unverifiable rumor. I suppose you can only try it to see if the rumor was true.

18

You Teach the Bible in Groups, Building on the Sermon

- ■ —Many pastors yearn for a chance to seriously discuss the sermons biblical text with members of the congregation.
- ■ —Thoughtful persons who have just heard a sermon often wish for an opportunity to question, clarify, or even disagree.
- ■ —This approach requires a preacher with the courage to openly "face the music."

Many is the time laypersons leave a worship service primed and ready to plunge into a discussion of the scripture that has just been the basis of the sermon in that service. This approach seeks to strengthen the congregation's involvement in, and attention to, that portion of the Bible used as the foundation and text of such a sermon.

Groups or classes are organized to study the same scripture used in a worship service, which has already been held, and in which most if not all of the participants have already been involved. Usually such programs meet immediately following the worship service, which is held before Sunday school. This approach has been used most often in my experience by newly organized churches, where classes are not already firmly set into particular patterns, with established teachers and curricula—although it need not be restricted to such situations.

Other churches, including those I have served, have had the groups meet on Sunday evening as a part of a program for the entire family. Sometimes called a Sunday evening fellowship, the evening starts with a covered dish dinner for the family, singing and fellowship around the tables, and then groups for each age, including the usual youth groups. In some churches this is followed by an evening worship service.

The key ingredients are three:

1. Hearing the pastor preach on a particular text.
2. Lay-led discussion of the text in small groups, and how the text was treated in the sermon.
3. An opportunity for the members of the congregation to question the preacher and to share their thoughts on the Scripture with the preacher.

PROCEDURE

1. The pastor preaches from and "works over" the biblical text in a worship service. The text may be from a lectionary, and it may or may not be announced in advance.

2. After hearing the pastor's use of the scripture, the adults of the congregation (and possibly the youth) meet in small groups or classes.

3. In each group the scripture is reread with each person in the group looking at a Bible if possible. Sometimes the text is read from more than one translation or paraphrase.

4. The groups then reflect on the scripture and the ways in which the preacher treated it. The participants offer their own insights and feelings concerning the text and may have questions they wish to address to the preacher.

At times there is a leader in each group who has studied the text in advance and who has sometimes met with the pastor and the other leaders to hear of the pastor's plans for treatment of the scripture in the sermon.

In other churches the leaders are not prepared beforehand, but know that their role is to guide the discussion,

123

help summarize the points of view, and pinpoint questions for the pastor.

The kinds of questions used in Depth Bible study or some other approach described in section 1 may be used in the groups to focus the discussion.

5. Finally, the groups are assembled for the final fifteen or twenty minutes of the period, and questions or comments are addressed to the preacher. He or she thus has the opportunity to hear the kinds of questions that have arisen in the minds of the congregation, to clarify ideas that were not clear, and to listen to other thoughts that have never occurred to other professional clergy-persons.

6. To stimulate discussion in the classes or groups, some pastors have used a sharp layperson who is prepared to be a Devil's advocate and who outlines what she or he heard in the sermon's treatment of the scripture. Then that person raises issues for the groups to discuss.

7. Another possibility is to have a copied outline of the treatment of the scripture in the sermon ready to be handed to the groups as they begin. This sheet may include some exegesis of key words in the text and some consideration of context.

ADDITIONAL COMMENTS

Such Bible teaching is often most helpful when it is done during a series of sermons on something such as the Apostles' Creed, the Lord's Prayer, or other basic aspects of the Christian faith.

Although some pastors have occasionally tried a "Dialogue Sermon," in which there is a planned conversation between the preacher and one or more persons during the worship service, this is difficult to construct and carry out helpfully. It has also been found that many people feel this is an inappropriate way to involve the congregation verbally in discussing the biblical text or sermon.

When using this approach to Bible teaching, it is important to keep the attention of the groups focused on the Scripture and the sermons treatment of it, and not get into discussing the minister's style or other facets of the sermon itself.

The morning worship service is the best-attended church event of the week, and when tied directly to small group study of the Scripture, this maximum attendance is utilized.

19

You Teach the Bible in a Worship Service

- ■ —The pastor stands directly in the rabbinical tradition of Jesus when worship is focused on scriptural study.
- ■ —Large numbers of members of our congregations never study the Bible or even think about it, except in a worship service.
- ■ —The impersonal atmosphere in a sanctuary is attractive to some persons as a place to learn.

"A little Bible study for a lot of people"

SOURCE AND DESCRIPTION

All worship services "teach" the Bible. The reading of scripture, the singing of hymns based on the Bible, prayers that use and refer to Scripture and, of course, the sermon based on Scripture—all teach the Bible to some degree. For most Christians, most of the time the worship service is the *only* teaching of the Bible to which they are regularly exposed.

Although the purpose of worship is focus on God, not on teaching men and women, the worship service nevertheless always contains teaching of the Scripture and the Christian faith.

In this approach, teaching takes a more central role in the worship service than usual, and the sermon is a "teaching sermon." Although it is certainly possible to do this in a Sunday morning service, it is more commonly used in a service at another time such as an evening service.

I have used this approach in both the smallest and the largest churches. In Houston at First United Methodist Church, two major series of these Bible teaching services were conducted with more than eight hundred persons in attendance on Sunday evenings. I also did this at the First United Methodist Church in Dallas, Texas. The procedure that follows was used in those two churches.

PROCEDURE

1. "The Entire Bible in Eight Sunday Nights" was the title of the most popular series. Based on the little book by Bernard Anderson, *The Unfolding Drama of the Bible,* this series gave a quick overview of the entire Bible using Anderson's three "Acts" of the Bible—Exodus, Exile, and Christ.

Although many would think that such a hasty survey treated the Bible without any chance of doing it justice, when balanced by other forms of Bible study, it serves a real need and has met with great appreciation.

A second series was entitled "The Ten Greatest Chapters of the Bible" and alternated between the Old and New Testaments. It was later extended because of great interest. A congregational "ballot" helped the pastor choose the chapters that were to be included. Some of the chapters we studied were:

John 1	Exodus 20
Psalm 8	Romans 8
Luke 4	II Samuel 12
Isaiah 53	I Corinthians 13
Matthew 5	I Corinthians 15

One of the Gospels can be studied in this fashion during Advent or Lent.

2. Equipment in a small church includes the pulpit and a large chalkboard. In a large church:

> A large movie screen, preferably one that can be drawn down from the ceiling.
> An overhead projector on a stand.
> A high stool for the pastor to sit at the projector, if desired.
> A portable, bandoleer microphone.
> Transparencies and marking pens.

3. The service is the usual one-hour-in-length and the "teaching sermon" is planned to take about thirty-five minutes of the service. Hymns, prayer, and special music all focus on the portion of Scripture to be studied.

4. The congregation is asked to bring their Bibles, and in addition, a 1-page sheet of Scripture is copied so that all can read in unison from the same translation. (This is not necessary, of course, if there are pew Bibles.)

5. The "teaching sermon" includes:

(a) Unison reading of Scripture (slowly and thoughtfully).

(b) Lecturettes (of about five minutes each) by the pastor, using the overhead projector or chalkboard to—

Outline.
Draw maps of the Holy Land, and so on.
Emphasize key words, ideas, persons, and events.
Summarize key ideas.

(I prefer to pre-prepare the transparencies on paper but not put the material on the transparency until during the teaching sermon. This is more interesting and lively than pre-prepared transparencies.)

(c) "Nudging your neighbor": Ask persons to turn to a partner—certainly no more than three persons talking together—to discuss carefully chosen questions that stimulate thought and involvement with the text. These discussions should be short, three to five minutes each. This can be done once or twice in one service.

Obviously it would be impossible to respond to many questions, which may arise during the discussions, although one or two may be considered.

Sometimes a question like, Was one of you talking to a person who seemed to have a particularly insightful response to the text? is useful. One or two of these responses could be included, but time should be controlled carefully.

(d) A summary that includes personal affirmation and witness by the pastor. It is helpful to put this summary and affirmation on the chalkboard, or on the overhead. (You may also want to have the summary for a hand out.)

6. There is an attempt, even in this short time and in a large formal setting, to include both information "About" the Scripture, and to have everyone become "Involved With" brief portions of the Scripture for a few minutes. This means that large portions of material are left out entirely (rather than briefly mentioned) and that time is taken for involvement with at least one carefully chosen brief section of the biblical text.

Following are samples of two transparencies from the third study of the "Entire Bible in Eight Sunday Nights." This third study covered the period of the judges, the major kings of Israel and Judah, and the preexilic prophets.

On the first sample there are parallel statements about

129

Judge
>   is not—a Judge.

Gideon
>   is—a military hero.

A Good King
>   is not—a "good" man.

David
>   is—a sinner who repents and accepts God's forgiveness.

Prophet
>   is not—one who correctly predicts the future.

Jeremiah
>   is—one who speaks for God.

Sample 2—Study 3

Conclusions

What does the past tell us?

- Faithfulness to God is Israel's security and salvation.

- *Rebellion brings ruin.*

- A prophet is right *even* when he reads the times incorrectly.

judges, kings, and prophets, and an example of each. In each instance there is an attempt to catch key ideas in a brief phrase.

Hand-printed rather than pre-typed material is much easier to read, gives emphasis to the ideas, and can be put up one idea at a time.

The second sample gives the conclusions of this third study, again in brief, direct, but encompassing phrases.

Again, even in so brief a time and looking at so much material, it is possible and very important that the participants be confronted personally at some point in the presentation, and feel themselves involved in the dialogue with God and themselves.

All pastors need to consider the needs of the larger congregation, who do not attend Sunday school classes, or Bible study groups for some form of Bible study. This is one possible way to meet part of that need. The further need of all Christians to get a "feel" for the sweep of the entire Bible must also be considered.

Such sessions, of course, risk utter superficiality, but they also offer considerable opportunities to entice the congregation into pursuing more significant forms of Bible study.

20

You Teach the Bible Through a Pastor's Bible Class

(A Model, not *the* Model)

- ■ —All congregations look to their pastor to teach them the Bible.
- ■ —Pastors who regularly teach a Bible class find rewards in their preaching and personal life.
- ■ —Such a class, even with a small enrollment, acts as leaven in the life of the congregation.

"Verse by Verse Through a Book"

A "Leaven" Bible class (for the congregation), which deals with every issue of life sooner or later.

Some variation of this approach is probably the most widely used throughout the world. The description that follows is of the way I have used this approach in a wide variety of churches from very small to very large. Every pastor will modify it in a number of ways.

For me this is serious, ongoing Bible study for those who will do weekly preparation in an

Open
Historical-Critical
Confrontational
Experiential

context.

132

To help insure that these qualities are visible in Bible study, I have developed some clear-cut principles over the years that I outline and discuss with the class early in the life of the group.

PRINCIPLES FOR BIBLE STUDY

1. The Word of God is Jesus Christ, and the words of the Bible tell us about that Word. Therefore, when we study the words of the Bible we always look behind, in, and through those words for God's Word—Jesus Christ.

2. No Christian has a monopoly on understanding either God's Word or the words of the scripture. This includes biblical scholars and the most unlearned Christian peasant. All of us must listen to one another as we seek to understand the richness of God's gifts.

3. We must assume everyone has Christian integrity and not accuse one another (no matter how unusual are the opinions) of being unchristian.

4. We must further assume that we will arrive at different understandings of portions of Scripture and that that will not disturb God as much as it will some of us.

5. Few of us will know Hebrew or Greek, and we therefore need to use a variety of English versions to try to understand the text.

6. While we accept differences between us, we do not feel that those differences are unimportant, or that they should be ignored or treated as if they did not matter.

7. Different biblical understandings can remain between us, but we can still be warm Christian friends. In fact, as we grow to better understand our differences, we can grow in our appreciation of one another.

(These principles were also included on page 102 of my earlier book, *Strengthening the Adult Sunday School Class*, published in 1981 by Abingdon.)

Some persons cannot agree with one or more of these "principles," so we simply accept that fact.

This Bible study meets weekly or biweekly, for one-and-a-half hours, beginning and ending on time. The leader is the pastor or, in a larger church, a minister on the staff, a theologically educated layperson, or possibly a former minister. Seating is at tables if at all possible.

A large group may meet in a large fellowship hall, with tables for one hundred or more if necessary or possible.

Persons remain at the same table week after week unless someone desires a change. The groups build up a sense of great community over the months.

All class members are expected to study the assigned scripture from one or more translations or paraphrases, and also to read one or more commentaries of their personal choice. Individuals develop their own favorite commentaries and become the "expert" on that commentary at their table, or for the entire class. The teacher makes sure several commentaries are available in the church library for those who do not wish to purchase their own.

The pastor usually needs to spend four to six hours preparing for each session, developing both content and procedure. Preaching can also be tied to this preparation. Sermons "jump out at you" all the way, including the class sessions themselves. In fact, this Bible study is usually enhanced by sermons that grow out of the same material.

Each study session includes from one verse to an entire chapter of a book, usually a commonly accepted pericope or about ten verses. There is no attempt to move quickly and full discussion of every verse takes place if it seems to be called for.

PROCEDURE

1. Assign the text in advance anticipating that it will be read and studied. Possibly assign specific types of

Small Group

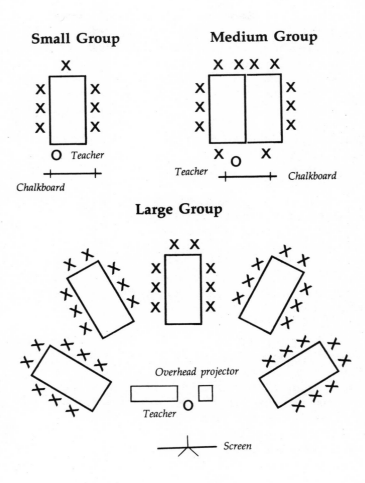

Medium Group

Large Group

Small Group

X

X   X
X   X
X   X

O   *Teacher*

Chalkboard

Medium Group

X X X X

X   X
X   X
X   X

X O X

Teacher   *Chalkboard*

Large Group

X X

X   X
X   X
X   X

Overhead projector

Teacher   O

Screen

preparation or questions dealing with particular aspects of the text.

2. Ask a member of the class to pray for insight and sensitivity.

3. Give a brief (ten- to fifteen-minute) illustrated lecture using a chalkboard or screen. You may want to draw maps, write key words, record central ideas, and so on. In this presentation the leader tries to bring the scripture passage into context by using standard "introduction" and exegetical material from a variety of sources and points of view. Questions for clarification are encouraged, and if someone has found a contrary opinion, it is freely expressed.

4. Assign questions for work at the table (from one to three questions). The questions are *confrontational, searching,* and if possible contain a *hook* that will "grab" attention. Be sure that no yes or no answers are possible.

Typical questions might be, How would more liberal or conservative Christians tend to view this passage differently? How would they explain their points of view? What are the values each point of view considers important? In what ways does this passage seem to confront today's church? confront you? Do you really believe in this kind of God? why? why not?

5. Ask persons to work in pairs, trios, or entire tables, depending on your "feel" of this situation and the nature of the questions. Work on the questions continues for ten to twenty minutes, occasionally thirty minutes. Class members may want to consult the commentaries they have with them as well as their Bibles.

It is usually best if the leader (a theologically educated person) does not take part in these small discussion groups, because many laypersons look upon the minister as the one with the correct answers.

6. Follow up with general discussion of the results of the small-group work. No groups or persons are called on to report. Emphasis is on interesting differences of interpretation or response.

No difficult question is ignored. Sharp differences of opinion are accepted and allowed to stand. It is usually best if the pastor refrains from giving personal opinions at this point because of "leader status," which could dampen the discussion of some persons in the group.

At the same time however, the leader "feeds in" various resources not commonly available to the participants, including notes from seminary, Bible courses, and so forth.

7. Follow up (if desirable) this general discussion with a more formal "mini-lecture" that brings in additional information and possibly introduces other theological viewpoints that have not been brought up in the class. The class is enriched if there is a search for spiritual values behind various points of view.

8. Be prepared for reactions, sometimes quite negative, which may be perhaps spoken in anger. Others may express strong affirmations.

This discussion may raise additional questions that may have to be delayed until the next session. The pastor may make specific assignments for research, such as, What were Martin Luther's views of this passage? or, What were John Wesley's?

9. Finally, give a summary of the session, including some personal thoughts and feelings such as, How my mind has changed over the years in regard to this part of scripture. When I was a leader of a class of this kind, I always tried to provide some appropriate affirmations of faith to close the evening.

10. Dismiss the class on time (one-and-a-half hours), but you may remain for individual or group discussion, which often borders on pastoral counseling.

ADDITIONAL COMMENTS

It is my experience that such Bible study will deal with every major theological issue and most personal problems over a period of a few weeks. Members of the class will want to reaffirm their faith, confess some persistent sins, vent anger at God, the church, and some ministers, and make new commitments to Christ. Future church leaders and Sunday school teachers will emerge as will those you find difficult to place in a church job.

Finally, you, the pastor, in the presence of a portion of the congregation, will put yourself in a position of *having* to study the Bible seriously. You will be surprised what this can do for your own spiritual life.

21

You Teach the Bible Using Bethel, Trinity, Kerygma, Disciple, or Other Long-term, High-commitment Series

- ■ —They include the *entire Bible*.
- ■ —They stress learning *facts*.
- ■ —They are taught by *trained teachers*.
- ■ —They are *long-term*—at least a year and often two.
- ■ —They require a *serious commitment*.
- ■ —They require *extensive homework*.
- ■ —They provide a *sense of accomplishment*.
- ■ —They are *different from Sunday school*.

In the last several years thousands of churches and more than a million adults and youth have enrolled in one of these Bible studies. These studies and others, like "Through the Bible in One Year" and "Word and Witness," have appealed greatly to a wide variety of churches in many denominations throughout the United States and several other countries.

I have chosen to describe four of these programs, and to offer some evaluative opinions on each. Many of the descriptions come directly from the materials themselves; others were made by those who have used them. The first three programs have been running for several years, and the fourth will be released for use in the fall of 1987.

I have visited several classes using *Bethel, Trinity*, and *Kerygma*, and was a member of the designing committee for

Disciple. I have read and studied the materials of each, although I have never led any of the studies myself.

BETHEL

■ —A series of six 7-week courses to be taught three a year for two years—a total of 42 lessons.

■ —The pastor or other key leaders go for two weeks of training to Madison, Wisconsin, in order to be able to train teachers for their own churches.

■ —Teachers enroll for eighteen months of training, which includes the same 42 lessons they will later teach to their own students. These training sessions last two-and-a-half hours each, one a week. All participants are laypersons who commit themselves not only to the training, but to then teach a class of their own for two years.

■ —Developed and written by the Reverend Harley Swiggum, a Lutheran minister more than twenty-five years ago, *Bethel* is by far the most used of these programs.

■ —For information, write or call:

Adult Christian Education Foundation
P.O. Box 8398
Madison, WI 53708
 ph. (608) 849-5933

Distinctive Features

■ —Consists of twenty-one lessons on the Old Testament and twenty-one lessons on the New Testament, using a workbook that includes homework, memorization, and Bible reading assignments.

■ —The teacher's book contains detailed lectures and

140

procedures, which the teachers are encouraged to follow closely.

■ —Stresses the learning of concepts far more than learning the narratives of the Bible. Concepts include ideas, prophecies, events, and even characteristics of a person like Joseph. (In my opinion, *Bethel* is overt, theological Bible study, with more emphasis on theological beliefs than on allowing the God of the Bible to live in your life.) As the publicity says, Bethel's goal "is to gain a deeper understanding of the Biblical message." Historical and literary materials are used in the prepared lectures to strengthen the message.

In the teaching materials, scripture references are pulled from many different books, piled one on top of another, to proof-text the case for one doctrine or another. Nevertheless, it is obvious that large numbers of ministers from many denominations have adapted Bethel to their own interpretations sufficiently to feel positive about its use.

■ —Strong emphasis on learning "About," with little or no interest in the participants getting "Involved With" the stories or text. (This is deliberate—the author believing one is a necessary prerequisite of the other.)

■ —Uses a distinctive set of 40 colorful "posters" to summarize the concepts of each chapter. These posters seek to work on the basis of association so that when you see the object, you think of the concept.

■ —As do many Christian Bible studies, *Bethel* comes dangerously close to "Christianizing" the Old Testament. For instance, on page 6 of lesson 1 of the New Testament book, we read: "The scattering of the Jews, *worked out by God,* in and through historical circumstances, save Paul and others like him from the necessity of proclaiming an unknown message in a foreign world. Truly God's hand had been everywhere, *shaping the course of history for the coming of Christ"* (emphasis mine).

■ —As the *Bethel* material says, it "leans toward the lecture method but does not discourage discussion."

■ —*Bethel* is the most expensive of the Bible studies examined here, owing in part to the cost of the training for two weeks in Madison, Wisconsin.

■ —The major goal of *Bethel* is "to secure a knowledgeable overview of the Scriptures to serve as a base from which to pursue an in-depth study of God's word." (In my experience, it has helped do just that for many.)

TRINITY

■ —A twenty-week survey of the entire Bible, ten weeks each for the Old and New Testaments, intended to be done in one year. This is to be followed by four additional years, each with two 10-week studies, as follows:

The Pentateuch and the Gospels
Joshua to Chronicles, and Acts to Galatians
Wisdom of Israel, and Ephesians to Hebrews
The Prophets, and James to Revelation.

■ —The teachers are expected to be theologically and biblically trained—ministers or well-trained laypersons.

■ —One and two-day training events are offered throughout the country, but attendance is not required to use the material (contrary to *Bethel*).

■ —*Trinity* was written and developed by Frank Warden, a United Methodist minister, who had been trained in

Bethel, and had led a large Bethel program for several years at Highland Park United Methodist Church in Dallas, Texas.

■ —For information, write or call:

TRINITY
El Paso, AR 72045
   ph. (501) 849-2131

Trinity has expanded rapidly to more than 8,000 churches in the United States, Korea, and other countries, and Dr. Warden is now its appointed full-time director.

Distinctive Features

■ —There are no leaders' guides. Trinity encourages each minister to develop his or her own.

■ —Notebooks for participants include an outline page for each book of the Bible, daily readings from the book being studied, questions to be answered for each reading, and meditation guides for personal use.

■ —There is a youth version of the program entitled *Choose Life,* with additional teaching suggestions.

■ —Audiotapes of Frank Warden's lectures if desired are available for purchase.

■ —Since there are no leaders' guides, teachers may use any procedures they wish, but there is a lot of material to be covered, leaving little time for much discussion unless there are two hours in each session (which is the suggested time).

■ —The concept of *trinity* (meaning three) is used through-out in a variety of ways:

   1. As an overall concept to help participants see the action of God as Creator, Son, and Holy Spirit.

2. As the three major levels or approaches to the biblical text—

    (a) Facts—The things the book being studied says.

    (b) Meaning—In *Trinity*, "meaning" is based on historical, cultural, and religious setting of time, but also includes what the author calls "eternal meaning in the facts of scripture." This is often a theological understanding of "faith history," but it is used so as to leave room for a variety of interpretations.

    (c) Application—Is highly personal in light of each participant's own life. The materials direct this application by a wide variety of probing questions.

3. As a three-point outline for each book of the Bible (except the minor prophets). These outlines are intended as tools for learning, but the threefold structure is obviously, on several biblical books, an arbitrary imposition.

■ —Cartoon figures and symbols like those in *Bethel* are used to assist participants in remembering key features of the various books. (The figures attempt to be both humorous and serious—a problem for some.)

■ —Although not prone to "Christianizing" the Old Testament, as does *Bethel*, *Trinity* does seem to assume that several Old Testament passages, such as Daniel 9:20-27 and Zechariah 11:12-13, correctly predict New Testament events (as did several New Testament authors).

■ —*Trinity* is growing rapidly in use because, as a pastor in Houston said, "I can shoot it through my own gun." That is its intention.

KERYGMA

■ —A 33-unit study focusing on the major themes of the Bible. Each session is designed for two hours to two-and-a-half hours.

There is a 3-session introduction to the Bible itself, followed by these ten themes:

God saves His people.
God is faithful to His people.
God's people think about Him.
God's people have leaders.
God's people have kings and a King.
God's law demands a righteous people.
God's people learn wisdom.
God's people worship.
God's people live in the world.
God's people have hope.

■ —Leaders (this program specifically prefers this term to "teachers") may be clergy or laypersons.

■ —There are two-day training workshops, which leaders are urged to attend and which include organizational matters and some practice leading the sessions.

■ —*Kerygma* was developed and written by James A. Walther, Sr., Professor of New Testament for more than thirty years at Pittsburgh Theological Seminary, and was first used at Southminster Presbyterian Church of that city. Later, *Kerygma* was used widely in the United Church of Canada.

Since its beginning, several other scholars and Christian educators, including Donald L. Griggs, have shared in redesigning the resources.

■ —For information, write or call:

KERYGMA
300 Mt. Lebanon Blvd.
Suite 205
Pittsburgh, PA 15234
   ph. (412) 344-6062

■ —*Kerygma* is growing rapidly, and is now used in more than 2,000 churches, including wide use in Canada and in American Baptist churches.

Distinctive Features:

■ —*Kerygma's* most distinctive feature is its *thematic* approach to the Bible, rather than being a book-to-book study. Participants follow the development of themes through the Old and New Testaments repeatedly, each time on a different "track." Its emphasis is to *"deal with the Bible whole, in contrast to the whole Bible"* (emphasis added).

■ —Places a major emphasis on the relationship of the Old and New Testaments, something that is often not understood by Christians.

■ —Provides extensive materials, including a resource notebook for participants and a leader's guide, which is full of suggestions for both content and procedures.

■ —Utilizes the full range of historical-critical and literary analysis of the Scriptures, far more than either *Bethel* or *Trinity*.

■ —Encourages great flexibility in educational procedures, and calls on major participation of those in the classes in a wide variety of ways.

■ —*Kerygma* encourages both learning "About" and "Involvement With" the texts of the Bible.

■ —*Kerygma* is also now producing additional studies, including *Interpretation. A Guide to Understanding the Bible Today* and *Shalom.*

■ —Cost of the program falls between *Bethel* and *Trinity*. This cost includes the cost of the materials and an enrollment fee for churches, which is based on their size.

■ —After completing the *Kerygma* studies, a layperson at the University United Methodist Church in Austin, Texas, said, "I have gained an overview of the Bible that enables me to understand the context of the scripture we read in the worship service."

■ —*Kerygma* demands serious study on the part of both leaders and participants, but users claim high rewards.

DISCIPLE

■ —A 34-week survey of the entire Bible, with a focus on deepening and strengthening the discipleship of every Christian through a greater working knowledge of the Bible. Two-hour classes, and three to four hours for study each week.

■ —Original format calls for pastors in local churches to teach the course to groups of twelve selected laypersons. It is expected the course will be repeated over the years, sometimes led by those who have taken it before.

■ —Designed by a representative group of consultants, this series is being coordinated by Bishop Richard Wilke, the United Methodist Bishop of Arkansas, and will be released in 1987 for use in the fall.

■ —For information, write or call:

DISCIPLE
The United Methodist Publishing House
201 Eighth Ave. S.
P.O. Box 801
Nashville, TN 37202
    ph. toll free (800) 251-8591

Distinctive Features

- —*Disciple* includes a one-session introduction, followed by fifteen sessions on the Old Testament, fifteen classes on the New Testament, and three sessions of summary, with emphasis on identifying and enabling the participants' strengths and talents for leadership.

- —Its purpose is to develop strong Christian leaders by way of in-depth study of the Scriptures.

- —There is a required three-day training workshop for pastors and key laypersons from congregations that vote to enroll in the program. These workshops are held in selected locations throughout the country.

- —A videotape segment is provided for each of the 34 sessions, featuring nationally known teachers and preachers.

- —A study guide is provided for each participant, and is also used by the teacher of trainers.

- —*Disciple* includes both a survey of selected passages, and a more in-depth consideration of a representative text each week.

- —The materials are intended to include learning "About" and to become "Involved With" the entire Bible.

- —Focus of these studies is always on each participant's growth in discipleship through serious Bible study.

22

You Teach the Bible, Developing Your Own Curriculum

- ■ —Many churches have developed and written their own curriculum, rather than using one of those described in chapter 21.
- ■ —Pastors and their staffs have found this experience amazingly beneficial to both them and the congregation.
- ■ —Using a curriculum in which the theological perspective meshes with that which is regularly preached unifies the church.
- ■ —Regular revision and adjustment is easier when you use your own material.

A pastor in Clear Lake, Texas, near the Johnson Space Center, tells a sobering story. A few years ago the church secretary was asked by an unknown lady, who came in one morning, if she could register for the weekly Bible class. The secretary began to tell the visitor about the several adult Sunday school classes that met regularly to study the Bible, but the woman said, "No—I mean a serious systematic Bible study taught by the pastor."

The secretary, somewhat confused by the unusual request, called the pastor and asked him to respond to the request directly. The stranger said, "I have just moved into this neighborhood, close to this church, in part so I could study the Bible, and learn more about it." The pastor was forced to confess that the church had no class of that type, but he vowed to himself that it would not be long before they did.

The woman never came back, but a few weeks later the pastor had developed a serious Bible study curriculum, which has transformed the life of that church.

During my research on this aspect of local church Bible study, I was surprised and later angered by a rather common response to my question, "What churches or pastors in your area teach the Bible regularly?"

The response too often was, "Well, Pastor _____ has evangelical leanings, and I've heard he teaches the Bible a good deal." Over and over it was implied that a self-conscious identification as an "evangelical" was a pre-condition for serious, pastor-led Bible study. Fortunately, this did not in fact prove to be true, but far too many pastors in mainline churches do not see regular, serious, systematic Bible study as part of their responsibility or opportunity.

Although I am sure there are hundreds of examples of Bible curriculum materials developed and written by individual local churches, I will briefly describe only three, all in the Houston area.

CLEAR LAKE BIBLE ACADEMY

For the past six years, Buddy Miller, the pastor of the Clear Lake United Methodist Church, has led a multifaceted Bible study program, which now enrolls more than three hundred persons. Pastor Miller does most of the teaching himself, and devotes a large portion of every week to the task. The church, with many from the U.S. space program in the congregation, has responded positively, and this minister gives Bible study a *high* priority.

In 1985, five courses were offered, the first course being given at three different times each week:

1. "Through the Bible in One Year"
2. "The Heart of Hebrew History"
3. "The Heart of the New Testament"
4. "Great Truths of the Bible"
5. "With Christ in the School of Prayer."

Course 1 is presupposed as a prerequisite for each of the other courses, and is offered on Sunday evening, Monday evening, and Thursday morning. The basic course, "Through the Bible in One Year," is based on a book of the same title by Alan Stringfellow, a Southern Baptist. This book is published by Virgil W. Hensley, of Tulsa, Oklahoma.

Pastor Miller says he adapts this book to his own point of view, and that of the United Methodist Church, when he feels it is needed. But he is enthusiastic about the overall helpfulness of the text.

Miller reports that he bases each course on a book, which is to be read by the participants, chapter by chapter, as the course goes along. He lectures on the same content, and allows considerable time for questions and answers. His classes are large, and there is no group discussion.

Miller writes, "I personally feel people are more receptive to studying the Bible than ever before. I am continually amazed at the numbers and faithful attendance in our classes here."

CHAPELWOOD COVENANT BIBLE STUDY
and
DISCIPLES BIBLE STUDY

Several years ago two neighboring United Methodist churches in Houston, first Chapelwood, and then Memorial Drive, decided that their churches needed serious, high-commitment Bible study. Several of their members had been an enthusiastic part of a large, independent group called the "Bible Study Fellowship," and these persons and others urged the staffs of these large churches to develop their own studies. Because of the enthusiasm for the format of the Bible Study Fellowship, both churches have adopted a modified form of that procedure, with the content written and shaped from their own denominational point of view.

The procedure is:

1. Assigned Bible readings to be done by each person in advance, with questions to answer and a commentary written by the staff to be read. About two hours of work is expected each week.

2. An hour-and-a-half weekly class, which includes:

    (a) A brief devotional (about 15 minutes) for the entire class, who meet together (sometimes one hundred or more).

    (b) Small group meetings of twelve to fifteen persons, with a lay leader who has attended a training session led by the staff. These groups meet for forty-five minutes, going over each of the assigned questions in turn, sharing and discussing their respective responses and answers.

        The assigned questions vary from asking for objective factual reporting to subjective opinion and reflection.

    (c) A general meeting of all the small groups for a 20-minute to 30-minute lecture by a staff member (usually an associate minister) that summarizes and pulls together the study for that week, and points toward the lesson for the next week.

    (d) The materials for the next week's lesson, which are then distributed.

—In each of these churches, several staff members take part in developing the materials and questions, including clergy and professional Christian educators.

—The course developed by these churches usually run from mid-September through April, all of that time being spent on the study of a single book. Books that have been studied so far include Luke, Isaiah, Acts, Genesis, Matthew, and Mark.

—The entire process is under constant evaluation and revision by the church staffs.

—For additional information, write:

Chapelwood Covenant Bible Study
Chapelwood United Methodist Church
11140 Greenbay
Houston, TX 77024

or

Disciples Bible Study
Memorial Drive United Methodist Church
12955 Memorial Dr.
Houston, TX 77024

—The staff members of both of these churches will testify to the large amount of work involved in developing your own curriculum, but will also attest to the very positive benefits to themselves and their congregations.

A few other congregations have now used these churches' material.

PART III

YOU ARE A CHRISTIAN EDUCATOR OR PASTOR: YOU TEACH AND TRAIN OTHERS TO TEACH THE BIBLE

- —In most local churches, the pastor is the only person who has formal training in the Bible and how to teach it.
- —If the pastor does not share that training and knowledge, it will never be known in that congregation.
- —In some large congregations there is both a pastor (sometimes several ministers) and one or more professional Christian educators who can share in the training of lay teachers. It needs to be cooperatively determined by the staff which persons can teach which aspects of Bible study the best.
- —Pastors and Christian educators may feel the need to receive more training in the Bible and how to teach it, at continuing education events.

23

You Teach the Use of Bible Helps

- ■ —Bible dictionaries, atlases, concordances, commentaries, and so on are vital to good Bible study.
- ■ —Few lay teachers have been taught how to use these helpful tools.
- ■ —Skills are best learned through guided practice, including the skillful use of Bible helps.

Never *tell* your teachers to use Bible helps. *Show* them how to use them, lead the teachers into their use, and these resources will become help indeed.

Bible helps or aids are primarily—

(a) A variety of Bible translations and paraphrases.
(b) Bible concordances
(c) Bible dictionaries
(d) Bible atlases
(e) One or more commentaries
(f) Topical concordances
(g) Gospel parallels

Often two or three of these types of resources will be included in the back of a Bible or published as a Bible handbook. All such handbooks are, of necessity, abridged. Here is a brief description of each:

(a) A variety of translations and paraphrases allow the English reader to better understand a text without knowledge of Hebrew or Greek, by careful comparison of various translations.

(b) A concordance allows you to find a particular verse, to find other verses where the same word is used, and to check additional meanings of a word in Greek and Hebrew dictionaries.

(c) A dictionary provides articles on biblical ideas, events, people, groups, and so forth, which enrich our understanding.

(d) An atlas (preferrably a historical atlas) gives us an understanding of changing boundaries, geographic features of the land, major movements of peoples, and especially a feeling for distance, elevation (depths of valleys and heights of hills), and climatic conditions.

(e) Commentaries provide information on who, when, where, to whom, and what of the biblical text, as well as suggesting of meanings and even applications.

(f) Topical concordances help you find all biblical references to a particular subject such as "forgiveness," whether or not the word itself appears in the scripture.

(g) Gospel parallels place the Gospels in parallel columns on the same page, allowing you to see, for example, one of Jesus parables in Matthew, Mark, and Luke, and possibly in John.

Merely telling the teachers this information, however, will not likely mean they will use these resources.

You must obtain the books (beg, borrow, or steal).
You must put the books in teachers' hands.
You must lead them into personally becoming familiar
   with the resources.

This means:

—You lead the congregation into buying as many of these resources as possible for the church library. (In larger churches there should be a shelf of these resources in each adult and youth classroom where there is a possibility they will be used.)

—You set up one or more workshops for teachers (teachers of children also) on the use of Bible helps. You call other churches and ministers in your city or county, and you borrow copies of the key resources so you have enough for all persons to be able to work in one or more.

WORKSHOP ON USE OF BIBLE HELPS #1

Time: An hour and a half.
Resources: A variety of Bible helps of each kind.
Tables for teachers to work in groups of three or four.
Leader: Pastor or professional educator.

Possible procedure:

1. Ask all persons to draw up a list of questions they and others have asked about the Bible, and after five minutes develop a composite list that may include:

Where is the verse that includes _____?
Who wrote that book?
Where is that place (geographically)?
What does that word mean?
What is the best translation of this?
What does the Bible say about _____?
How can I find everything about _____?
When was this written?
What proof do we have for this?
How do you pronounce this?

159

2. Divide the workshop into work groups of three or four with at least one copy of each major resource in each group.

Caution—Do not try to include more people than can share and work in each type of resource.

3. Lead the work groups to find answers to selected questions; for example:

(a) Where can I find "habitat"? Everyone turns to a concordance and looks in the alphabetical list and does not find it; it is a modern word. But they do find "habitation" appearing in both the Old and New Testaments.

Compare the different ways the word is used in different texts.

If you have a *Strong's* or *Young's* concordance, follow the number after the verses to the back, where the Greek or Hebrew dictionary is located. There you will find other possible meanings of the word.

(b) What can I find in the Bible about "forgiveness"?

First check a regular concordance as in question 1. Then check a topical concordance under the heading "Forgiveness."

(c) How can I find out more about the Pharisees?

Use a Bible dictionary. Here you will find one or more pages on the Pharisees (probably more than you want to know!). A good Bible dictionary will give you a historical perspective on the subject.

(d) Where did the Exodus take place? Use a Bible atlas. You will find one or more maps.

Also, a Bible dictionary will often overlap this information.

(e) What does that section of scripture mean? Who wrote it? when? to whom? Use a commentary. All commentaries include three types of material, this way whether they are divided or not:

Introduction: Who? to whom? when? where? why? what?

Exegesis: A word study that examines context, style, and so on in order to be as precise as possible.

Exposition: Interprets and expounds the text, often with suggested application.

(f) How is this passage translated in a number of different Bibles? Choose a biblical passage and have the groups look at:

King James Version
Revised Standard Version
The New English Bible
The Living Bible (Paraphrase)
J. B. Phillips (Paraphrase)

Notice the differences. Are there implications raised by any of these differences? If so, check one or more commentaries for the passage.

Warning: All Bible helps, of whatever type, have a theological point of view, whether they state it or not. This is to be expected and should not be a concern. You should just be aware that it is there.

The theological point of view is, of course, most apparent in commentaries, and least in concordances. Atlases and dictionaries often have distinct points of view as well.

I find it valuable in teaching to have read about and been aware of more than one theological viewpoint.

WORKSHOP #2

Most teachers will feel they have only "gotten their feet wet" in the process of the first workshop and will realize they need other supervised experiences to be able to use

Bible helps skillfully. Workshop #2 helps them continue to build this skill.

Using Learning Centers

Have five different tables, each with one Bible help and directions for using that resource.

Table 1—Concordance and topical concordance
Table 2—Bible dictionary
Table 3—Bible atlas
Table 4—Bible commentary
Table 5—Several Bible translations and paraphrases

Have another direction sheet at each table that uses the same kind of search exercises as in workshop #1. Give persons at least ten to fifteen minutes to work at each table, and then have them go to another. Persons can start at any table and move in any order. One or more leaders should circulate and help anyone who is having a problem.

These workshops can be followed over the succeeding months by calling attention to what is obtained from such resources for various Sunday school lessons.

Finally, you must learn to use the resources yourself, and use them! This is a skill, and skill comes only with practice.

24

You Teach Teachers to Use the Bible in the Sunday School Lesson

■ —Teachers sometimes believe that the more Bible verses they read, the more the class has studied the Bible.

■ —Teachers must actually take part in different approaches to develop confidence in using these approaches.

■ —The pastor or professional Christian educator has the responsibility to lead these experiences.

Sunday school lessons are full of the Bible, but many persons who come go home week after week without getting involved with the Scripture itself.

Strangely, one of the reasons is that many lessons cover too much of the Bible, too quickly, and too casually. Much Sunday school material is sprinkled with several scripture passages on every page. The writers and editors seem bent on proving that they believe in the Bible by quoting it in every direction.

Such use of the Bible in Sunday school lessons prevents the class from getting involved with any one portion of the Bible in any depth. Teachers must be trained to pick from the many portions of the Bible, and to divide the long sections of the scripture, thus concentrating on a limited number of verses. In this way teachers will be trained to study the Bible seriously, rather than casually.

STUDY THE BIBLICAL MATERIAL FOR THE COMING QUARTER

One of the most rewarding ways to enrich and enable good teaching is for the Christian educator or pastor to volunteer to meet at the beginning of a quarter with (for example) the teachers of junior highs and go over the biblical material for the coming thirteen lessons. This means, of course, that the pastor or Christian educator will have to spend several hours preparing for the sessions. He or she will need to gather a variety of Bible helps, such as a Bible dictionary, Bible atlas, and some commentaries, to search for clarity on the biblical material under consideration, and also gather additional enriching information for the unit itself. (You will be surprised when you do this at how much you learn yourself!)

Although provision of additional material "About" is of great importance, teachers also need to experience getting "Involved With" the biblical text. Telling them about getting involved will not do it. The teachers must experience one or more approaches that actually involve them.

Thus a portion of your training session should be spent demonstrating one or more approaches, either from the denominational material for teachers, or from a book like this.

You need the experience, the teachers need the experience, the youth and adults need the experience. You provide the experience.

SERIES OF DEMONSTRATIONS OF APPROACHES TO BIBLE STUDY

All teachers want to feel they are doing a good job. Self-confidence, that one knows what one is doing, helps a great deal in doing a good job. Self-confidence comes from experience. Training provides the experience.

Many teachers resist going to training opportunities beyond the local church. District, Regional, Presbytery, Conference, and Diocesian events are quite suspect for teachers who have been "burned" by poor events in the past. They also know that pastors and Christian educators have been known to stretch the truth in regard to the quality of forthcoming events. You have to overcome their "bunk" detectors. A good training event needs—

- ■—Focus
- ■—Practicality
- ■—Demonstration
- ■—Experience.

Plan four demonstrations of approaches to Bible study. The four might include:

1. Depth Bible study
2. Praxis Bible study
3. Theological Bible study
4. Paraphrase and Reverse Paraphrase Bible study, or others.

Do one approach in each session and allow one hour and a half for each event.

Demonstrate, do not describe, the approach being used, and discuss and evaluate the experience when it is completed.

The teachers in your church will be grateful.
You will learn as much as they do.
The possibilities for enhancement of Christian faith will be present.

25

You Teach the Bible Yourself, so You Will Not Die in the Faith

- ■ —The nuts and bolts of the church are deadly if they are not regularly lubricated with the Good News of the gospel.
- ■ —The organizational demands of the church and the needs of the congregation can eat up the spiritual reserves of every church professional.
- ■ —The regular infusion of group Bible study goes a long way toward keeping the spirit of Jesus Christ alive in our minds and hearts.
- ■ —Agreeing to teach a Bible class of adults or youth helps keep us honest in regard to our commitment to continuing to "grow in the Lord."
- ■ —The biblical knowledge and training we have received from seminary and other events demands to be shared with those whom the church has called us to serve.
- ■ —"Ignorance of the Scriptures Is Ignorance of Christ."
  —Jerome

Summary

1. The Bible is the book of the church, and it belongs to every Christian. The God of the Bible is our God, and we look through every page of the Bible for God Himself.

2. All members of the church are called on to study and learn the Bible because it is the primary written witness to the love of God we know in Jesus Christ.

3. We teach the Bible with both our minds and our hearts, seeking for mental and emotional insights.

4. Such teaching results in learning more *about* the Bible, as well as leading us to become *involved with* the biblical stories and characters themselves.

5. All methods and procedures commonly used in education, such as story-telling, lectures, discussion, and so on, have a function to perform in teaching the Bible when used in balance with other methods.

6. Depth Bible study helps us move from objective understanding of the text, to subjective involvement with the Scripture ourselves.

7. Theological Bible study helps us ask the key theological questions about God, ourselves, and the relationship between God and His creatures.

8. Shared Praxis Bible study pushes us as teachers to examine carefully the reasons for and implications of our actions for and the intersection between the biblical story and vision, and our stories.

9. Dialogue and Encounter Bible study forces us to ask hard, critical, analytical questions, as well as opening our eyes and feelings to the call of God within its words.

10. Sensory-Transforming Bible study invites us to use all our senses—hearing, seeing, smelling, touching, and tasting—to work our way into the inner dynamic of biblical stories, and to imagine ourselves as part of the interaction and demand of the narrative.

11. Spectrum Bible study helps us realize how differently Christians understand a particular text, and leads us to examine their reasoning for their position.

12. In Paraphrasing and Reverse Paraphrasing, the teacher leads the participants to put the biblical text in their own words, and to look at some of the negative roots of the Bible's most positive statements.

13. In memorizing key portions of the Bible, Christian students find themselves with an enlarged Bible of their own in their heads, rather than on their shelves.

14. Using the knowledge and dynamic of biblical scholars on audio and videotapes can enhance our teaching when such tapes are "kept in their place."

15. Youth *can* and *want* both to know more about the Bible and to become involved with the Bible when they are led into the text creatively and lovingly.

16. Videotapes and biblical films can make the narrative of the Bible vivid and memorable, but classes should be "debriefed" on the tendency of these resources to interpret the Bible too literally.

17. Using a variety of dramatic ways to involve our pupils in the biblical text can help "the entire person"—intellectually and emotionally—participate in the biblical drama.

18. The good Bible teacher selects from and brings together the various approaches available for interesting and exciting lessons.

19. Pastors enhance their sermons by organizing the congregation into study groups to study the biblical text before it is preached.

20. Some brave preachers enlist a serious, purposeful

group of laypersons to share in the biblical preparation of their sermons.

21. Other pastors organize groups to discuss the biblical text after they have preached on that passage, to deepen the participants' understanding.

22. Pastors involve many persons in some Bible study in worship services, while also providing in-depth Bible study for a few who want to work quite hard in a pastor's Bible class.

23. Interested pastors use one of the available systematic prepackaged Bible studies that are available, or they develop their own curriculum of this type, enlisting sizable numbers from the congregation.

24. Pastors and Christian educators teach Sunday school teachers and others how to use concordances, commentaries, Bible dictionaries, and atlases, as well as how to improve their teaching of the Bible in their lessons.

25. Pastors and Christian educators teach Bible classes themselves for the sake of their own spiritual life.

Suggestions for Using This Book

As a Teacher:

Start at the back. Read the twenty-five conclusions—see what sounds interesting, challenging. Read the Introduction and then the chapter that describes in more detail the approach you find interesting.

Plan to try that approach. Tell the class you are using something new to you, smile, and say, "Let's try it." Later, evaluate, modify, and try another approach.

As a Trainer:

Announce an evening of using Bible study methods for adults and youth. Actually *do* one or two approaches, rather than talk about several. A month later, do two other approaches.

Ask your church to buy a copy of this book for each teacher of adults and youth, in appreciation of their desire to grow in service to God and their pupils.

As a Pastor:

In addition to the two suggestions above, try one of the seven approaches suggested as possibilities for the pastor. Consider the values and the commitment of time. Enrich the study of the Bible for yourself and your congregation.

Annotated Bibliography

The Bible and Bible Study

Anderson, Bernhard W. *The Unfolding Drama of the Bible*. New York: Association Press, 1957.
A very imaginative and helpful summary of the Bible and its major events and concepts.

Barr, James. *The Scope and Authority of the Bible*. Philadelphia: Westminster Press, 1980.

Bird, Phyllis A. *The Bible As the Church's Book*. Philadelphia: Westminster Press, 1981.

Brown, Robert McAfee. *The Bible Speaks to You*. Philadelphia: Westminster Press, 1965.
Centers on the central themes and emphasis of the Bible. Clear and forceful. Has been reprinted several times. Was originally written for high school youth.

Brueggemann, Walter. *The Creative Word: Canon As a Model for Biblical Education*. Philadelphia: Fortress Press, 1982.
Calls for education to pay attention to "The Torah of the Priest," "The Counsel of the Wise," and "The Word of the Prophet."

Craddock, Fred B. *Overhearing the Gospel*. Nashville: Abingdon, 1978.
An important book for teaching the Bible.

DeDietrich, Suzanne. *God's Unfolding Purpose: A Guide to the Study of the Bible*. Trans. Robert McAfee Brown. Philadelphia: Westminster Press, 1960.
A "Salvation History" approach to Bible study.

Griggs, Donald L. *Praying and Teaching the Psalms*. Nashville: Abingdon Press, 1984.
An extremely creative treatment of the study of the Psalms for serious adult or youth.

Jordan, C. Ferris. *Bible Teaching for Adults Through the Sunday School*. Nashville: Convention Press, 1984.
A useful Southern Baptist text.

Maas, Robin. *Church Bible Study Handbook*. Nashville: Abingdon, 1982.
Outlines a complete plan for teaching exegesis to laypersons in a congregation. Very specific and helpful.

Rahtjen, Bruce D. *Biblical Truth and Modern Man: A Layman's Guide to Understanding the Bible*. Nashville/New York: Abingdon Press, 1968.

Russell, Letty M., (ed.). *Feminist Interpretation of the Bible*. Philadelphia: Westminster Press, 1985.

    See especially chapter 9, "Feminist Interpretation: A Method of Correlation," by Romary Radford Ruether.

Ryan, Roy H. *Planning and Leading Bible Study*. Nashville: Discipleship Resources, 1973.

    If you can still find a copy, this is a very useful book on teaching the Bible.

Smart, James D. *The Strange Silence of the Bible in the Church: A Study in Hermeneutics*. Philadelphia: Westminster Press, 1940.

    Still raises many key issues in a forceful way.

Weber, Hans-Ruedi. *Experiments with Bible Study*. Philadelphia: Westminster Press, 1981.

    Possibly the best book on Bible study in print. Includes many models of creative Bible study.

Adult Christian Education

Little, Sara. *To Set One's Heart: Belief and Teaching in the Church*. Atlanta: John Knox Press, 1983.

    One of the most thoughtful and helpful books written on the methods and contribution of teaching for belief.

McKenzie, Leon. *The Religious Education of Adults*. Birmingham: Religious Education Press, 1982.

    A valuable overview of adult religious education. Does not consider adult Sunday school classes.

Murray, Dick. *Strengthening the Adult Sunday School Class*. Nashville: Abingdon, 1981.

    See especially section III.

Peterson, Gilbert A., (ed.). *The Christian Education of Adults*. Chicago: Moody Press, 1984.

    A self-described "evangelical" book, its understanding of teaching adults is helpful to all. See especially chapter 6.

Teaching the Bible to Youth

Gobbel, A. Roger, Gertrude G. Gobbel, and Thomas E. Ridenhour, Sr. *Helping Youth Interpret the Bible*. Atlanta: John Knox Press, 1984.

Griggs, Donald L. *20 New Ways of Teaching the Bible*. Nashville: Abingdon, 1977.

Hestenes, Roberta. *Using the Bible in Groups*. Philadelphia: Westminster Press, 1983.

Lohfink, Gerhard. *The Bible: Now I Get It—A Form Criticism Handbook*. New York: Doubleday and Co., 1979.

Metcalf, William. *16 Methods of Group Bible Study*. Valley Forge, Pa.: Judson Press, 1980.

Smith, Judy Gattis. *20 Ways to Use Drama in Teaching the Bible.* Nashville/New York: Abingdon Press, 1975.

Stone, J. David, (ed.). *The Complete Youth Ministries Handbook.* Nashville: Abingdon, 1979.

  See chapter 5, "Creating and Leading Experiential Bible Study for Youth," by Marion Bontrager.

————. *Catching the Rainbow: Complete Youth Ministries Handbook,* vol. 2. Nashville: Abingdon, 1981.

  See chapter 9, "Biblical Mimodrama," by Bryan Humphrey.

Distinctive Approaches to Bible Study

Groome, Thomas, *Christian Religious Education: Sharing Our Story and Vision*. San Francisco: Harper and Row, Publishers, 1980.

  Describes Praxis Bible study.

Power, W. J. A. "The Book of Genesis, A Folk Theology," *Perkins Journal,* (Winter 1984), Southern Methodist University, Dallas, Texas.

————."Once upon a Time: Discovering Your Story in Biblical Stories." Two audiotapes, Thesis, P.O. Box 11724, Pittsburgh, PA.

Wainwright, Arthur. *Beyond Biblical Criticism: Encountering Jesus in Scripture.* Atlanta: John Knox Press, 1982.

  Advocates and demonstrates a "Faith" approach to the Bible.

Wink, Walter. *Transforming Bible Study: A Leaders' Guide*. Nashville: Abingdon, 1980.